"A Good Name Is Rather To Be Chosen Than Great Riches"

Proverbs 22:1

By Marjorie A. Glemaker

*All scriptures taken from
the King James Version of the Bible,
unless otherwise indicated.*

Copyright © 1986 By Marjorie A. Glemaker
All rights reserved.
Silhouettes and Artwork, By Carletta Keith
Printed in United States of America
Library of Congress Catalog No.: 0961836903
Typography and Design - Faith Designs, Inc.
Fayetteville, North Carolina
ISBN# 0-9618369-0-3

No part of this book may be duplicated in any shape, form or manner without express written permission of the author.

Dedication

With love and appreciation to my Lord and Savior Jesus Christ, who loves us so much He gave His life for our sin, so God the Father could see His children in the Righteousness of Christ. It was the Love of Jesus that inspired me to write this book, to draw us closer to God and prepare for the coming of Christ to receive as His own, a Holy people.

Table of Contents

Introduction V

The Kingdom of God 2

Jesus Means Savior 4

My Children 6

Names 7

Index of Names 8-34

About the Author 185

About the Artist 186

Introduction

Each name is written in the righteousness of Christ and how the Father sees you in perfection; but remember, we are not yet perfect here in this world, only reaching for the goal. These poems are written to God's children. "For as many as are led by the Spirit of God, they are the children of God." Are you being led by the Spirit of God?

The fruits of your name will show in your life, if you walk after the Spirit of God and his righteousness. The closer you walk with God, the closer you grow in righteousness because of Christ Jesus. You can do all things through Christ who strengthens you.

God inspired me to write these poems for us to see that He loves us where we are. We need to love God more, for He is the One who created love from the beginning. Our God should have the first place in our hearts, our minds and our souls.

The Kingdom of God is within . . .

The Kingdom of God

Are you a Christian, a child of God?

A Christian believes in God, that He is our Father and He walked the earth through Jesus His only begotten son, man without sin; born of a virgin.

He was born for the very purpose to draw all men unto Him and to die for all sins of the world. For all have sinned and come short of the Glory of God.

We must repent and be sorry for our sins and ask Jesus to forgive us from our sins, we need to forgive others that Jesus will forgive us. Then Jesus gives us eternal life in heaven forever, our spirit shall never die but live throughout eternity. It's so simple to be a child of God, but some grow hard hearted and will not confess their sins and say they are sorry. But this must be done in order to be a Christian; we need to tell Jesus we are sorry for our sins because He chose to die for us.

When is this done, a new life appears in the Christian, the old nature begins to pass away and their spirit comes alive to the things of God and his righteousness. We can repent anywhere and be sorry for it will be in truth and in spirit. God always hears a forgiving heart. The Kingdom of God in within each person.

Are you in His Kingdom? God dwells in us today; if we are a Christian. His Holy Temple.

Salvation

Jesus Means Savior

But what few believe it? Who will listen? To whom does God reveal His open arms to save? To all who receive Jesus, God's only begotten Son. Jesus will grow like a tender plant among dry ground, sprouting green shoots from the root. That's the way God sees Jesus. But men from the world see Him as unattractive, nothing to be desired or want His way of life, none desire to take His place.

We despised Him and rejected Him, a man of sorrows, who knew grief. We hid our face from Him and lifted Him not up when people despised and rejected Him; even when His grief was for our sorrows, we did not lift Him up, so He was bruised and wounded for our chastisement. Our peace was upon Him, along with the lashes He took for us that we might be healed today.

We are the ones who walked away as sheep stray, to follow our own way. Jesus carried the guilt and sins of every one of us. We walked away from Him, His way, His truth, and His life.

Jesus became oppressed and afflicted, yet He opened not His mouth, never said a word, He was brought as a lamb to be slaughtered, dumb, silent before the very people who condemn Him.

From prison and trial we led Him away to His death, but who among us realized it was for us He died. For our sins He suffered our punishment. What we really deserved, He carried the cross.

Jesus was crucified like a criminal to death, yet after death lay in a rich man's tomb. He spoke no evil of anyone. He never did wrong to anyone, there was no deceit in His mouth, neither in His heart against no man.

It was the Lord Jesus who was bruised and grieved, yet pleased by His own will to offer up His life for our sins. Because of this, He shall see His seed and many heirs to live a prolonged life, the pleasure of the Lord will prosper.

He shall see the travail of His soul and be satisfied by His knowledge of righteousness to justify many, to carry their sins before God. Jesus will be counted righteous and honored before God, be He poured out his soul unto death. But He was counted a sinner among men to the people of the world while He hung on the cross. Yet Jesus pleads with God for all sinners these very words, "Father forgive them for they know not what they do," "Father forgive them," is still His plea.

"For He shall give the angels charge over thee to keep thee in thy way."

Psalm 91:11

My Children

It is the Lord who speaks to you, the one who sits on the circle of the earth. I created the heavens and stretched out a veil above the earth and tore it down so you could see the truth. Who can you compare with me? Who is my equal? I am the Holy One and call each of you by name. There is no excuse for you, to who I am your God, to know the truth and righteousness and not do it. You have your heart on the blessings that I can give you, but I say seek me, love me, learn of me. For I love you and I know your thoughts and your hearts are not completely on me. You need not ask for blessings for my children are blessed people. Give me your time and learn of me, sit with me, be still and seek to learn the depth of me. I created love and want to teach you to love me with all of your heart, all of your soul and all of your might. I love you, my children. I am the Lord, your God, and the Holy One who lives forever.

These are the words God gave me, which inspired me to write this book by His Spirit.

MAG

Names

Names are special and we all have a name to identify who we are. Your name will follow you forever. Names have meaning with character and traits. Do you live up to your name? A good name is rather to be chosen than great riches (Proverbs 22:1). You will be remembered by your name throughout eternity. The Lord inspired me to write this book with a personal love for each one of His children, to bring wisdom, hope and encouragement to His own, and to use me as an instrument of His love to you. Some of these writings He gave me wisdom, to share with individuals for strength to be a conqueror over weaknesses; and others He wanted to encourage and to give hope. These are Christian poems given by God to His own, who believe in Christ, His only begotten Son and one day we will all be with Him and in His oneness. It's my prayer you will enjoy this book. It was my personal pleasure to relate this book to you for the Glory of our Father and draw myself and you nearer to Him. I have already been drawn to see His deep love for us and an unending presence of Him.

Index

Name	Character	Page
Aaron	Bringer of Light	150
Abbott - Abbot	Benevolent	116
Abel	Full of Life	154
Abigail	Source of Joy	108
Abner	Trustworthy	64
Abraham - Abram	Righteous Protector	142
Ada	Happy Spirit	52
Adam	God's Creation	40
Adeline	Woman of Esteem	78
Adella	Woman of Esteem	78
Adelle - Adele	Devoted Heart	66
Adolph - Adolf	Courageous Spirit	120
Adrian	Diligent Worker	70
Agatha	A Good Heart	116
Agnes	Pure One	132
Alan - Allen	Refreshing One	154
Albert - Al	Man of Honor	122
Alberta	Noble One	122
Aldrich	Full of Wisdom	180
Alexander - Alex	Brave Protector	142
Alexandria	Secure Spirits	156
Alexis	Secure Spirits	156
Alfred	Good Counselor	44
Alice	Truthful	172
Alicia	Truthful	172
Alisa - Alica	Truthful	172
Allison - Alison	Truthful	172
Alma	Kind and Loving	116
Almer	Kind and Loving	116
Aloph - Alaph	Peaceful Spirit	120
Alpha	Chosen One	40
Alta	Pure One	136
Alton	Resourceful	154
Alvera	Excellent Spirit	80

Index

Name	Character	Page
Alvin	Noble	38
Amanda	Beloved	44
Amber	Precious One	132
Ambrose	Enduring	88
Amelia	Diligent	70
Amos	Compassionate	90
Ampy	Compassionate	90
Amy	Beloved	44
Andrea - Andria	A Godly Woman	166
Andrew	Strong Manly	164
Andy	God's Strength	164
Angela	Bringer of Truth	172
Angus	Creative Spirit	148
Anita	Gracious One	104
Ann - Anne	Gracious One	104
Anna - Annie	Gracious One	104
Annette - Anette	Gracious One	104
Anthony - Antony	Priceless One	138
Antoinette	Gracious One	104
Antonia	Gracious One	104
Antonio - Tony	Priceless One	138
April - Apryl	New Faith	70
Ardelle	Devoted Heart	66
Arlen	Faithful	82
Arlene - Arleen	Faithful	82
Arnold	Brave and Strong	46
Arron	Exalted	138
Arthur	Man of Integrity	72
Artis	God's Glory	40
Ashley	Prosperous One	92
Ashton	Prosperous One	92
Aubrey	Leader	46
Auderia	Noble Strength	102
Audrey - Audey	Noble Strength	102

Index

Name	Character	Page
Augustine	Consecrated to God	58
Augustus	Man of Distinction	138
Auora - Arora	Morning Light	52
Avery	Good Counselor	44
Ava	Gracious	58
Avon	Generous One	90
Barbara - Babs	Coming with Joy	54
Barbel - Barble	Coming with Joy	54
Barlett - Barlette	Delightful One	70
Barnaby	Reverent Spirit	66
Barney	Mighty and Powerful	120
Barry	Courageous	134
Bartholomew	Industrious	92
Bea	Bringer of Joy	54
Beatrice	Bringer of Joy	54
Belva	Inner Beauty	106
Benedict	Blessed by God	82
Benjamin	Favored Son	138
Bennett - Bennette	Joyful Spirit	54
Benita - Bennita	Victorious	166
Bernadette	Womanly	166
Bernard	Mighty and Powerful	134
Bernice	Victorious	112
Bernita	Victorious	112
Bert	Honored	150
Bertha	Bright One	150
Bessie - Betsy	Consecrated unto God	58
Beth	Abiding with God	36
Bethany	Grateful Spirit	36
Betty	Pure One	58
Beulah	Faithful One	82
Beverly	Diligent	70
Billie Jean	Humble	48
Blaine	God's Strength	64

Index

Name	Character	Page
Blaire - Blair	God's Strength	64
Blake	Pure One	96
Blanche	Purity	146
Blythe	Joyous	108
Bonita - Bonnie	Sweet and Fair	106
Boris	Loyal	118
Boyd	Brave	46
Bradley	Abundant Power	96
Branton	Strong in Victory	134
Breck	God's Princess	102
Brenda	Enthusiastic	118
Brendon	Strong in Victory	134
Brent	Rising Above	120
Brett	Loyal	118
Brette	Loyal	118
Brian - Brien	Strong in Virtue	72
Bridgette	Strong Heart	168
Brigette	Victorious Spirit	112
Brittany	Victorious Spirit	112
Brooke	Refreshing One	52
Bruce	Secure One	156
Bruno	Loving One	116
Bud	Strong, Priceless	138
Bunnie	Victorious	112
Burney	Victorious	176
Burton - Burt	Abundant Power	120
Byron	In Full Strength	70
Cacey - Casey	Transformed Heart	168
Caleb	Courageous	46
Candace - Candice	Woman of Honor	122
Candy	Woman of Honor	122
Carl	Strong Manly	164
Carla	Strong Womanly	166
Carletta	Strong Woman	166

Index

Name	Character	Page
Carman	Song of Joy	160
Carmella	Gentle	90
Carmillia	Victorious	112
Carmine	Living in Harmony	90
Carol	Song of Joy	160
Carolina - Karoline	Refreshing Joy	166
Carrie	Strong Womanly	166
Carter	Lifter of Ears	64
Catherine - Katherine	Pure	146
Cathleen - Kathleen	Pure	146
Catrina - Katrina	Pure	146
Catrisse	Loving	48
Cecil	Humble Spirit	72
Cecillia	Humble Spirit	72
Chad	Defender	142
Charissa	Full of Grace	104
Charity	Loving	48
Charlene	Womanly	166
Charles-Chuck-Charlie	Strong Manly	138
Charlotte - Charlette	Full of Grace	104
Cheri	Cherished One	136
Cherise	Cherished One	136
Cheryl	Womanly	166
Chester	Strong Defender	142
Chico	Living in Freedom	156
Chris	Follower of Christ	86
Christella	Follower of Christ	86
Christian - Kristian	Follower of Christ	86
Christina - Kristina	Follower of Christ	86
Christine - Kristine	Follower of Christ	86
Christoffer	Follower of Christ	86
Cie	Humble Spirit	72
Claire - Clair	Bringer of Light	160
Clara	Pure in Grace	104

Index

Name	Character	Page
Clarence	Strong Character	138
Clark	Full of Wisdom	180
Claude	Full of Humility	48
Claudette	Full of Humility	48
Clayton	God's Mold	66
Clement	Kind One	116
Cleo	Kind One	116
Clifford	Viligant	76
Clinton	Full of Forgiveness	116
Clyde	Of Good Report	62
Coleen - Colleen	Victorious Spirit	96
Colette - Collette	Victorious Spirit	112
Conrad	Full of Wisdom	180
Conway	Full of Wisdom	180
Constance - Connie	Devoted Spirit	38
Cooper	Prosperous	106
Corbet - Corbit	Diligent	76
Cormella - Carmella	Victorious Spirit	96
Cornelius	Vigilant	178
Courtney	Woman of Distinction	46
Craig	Strong Enduring	74
Cristal	Follower of Christ	86
Cristine	Follower of Christ	86
Currie - Curry	Hero	62
Curtis	Courteous One	62
Cynthia	Reflector of Light	15
Dale	Courageous	120
Dana	Industrious Spirit	9
Danette	Pure One	140
Daniel-Dan-Danny	God is Judge	9
Danielle	God is Judge	140
Daphine	Devoted One	6
Darby	Freedom	15
Darcy - Darci	Crowned	62

Index

Name	Character	Page
Dari - Darie	Compassionate	90
Darla	Tenderly Loved	44
Darlene	Tenderly Loved	44
Darren - Darrin	Blessed in Bounty	132
Darwin	Man of Esteem	78
David	Beloved	44
Dawn	Joy and Praise	54
Dawson	Gift of God	94
Dean	Courageous	46
Deana - Deanna	Courageous	102
Deborah - Debra	Seeking One	158
Delia - Delilah	Delightful One	136
Delmar - Delma	Resourceful	158
Delores - Dee	Compassionate Spirit	88
Delton	Loving	136
Deneal	Champion	112
Denise	Wise Discerner	72
Dennis	Wise Discerner	72
Derek - Derrick	Full of Justice	96
Desirae - Desree	Beloved	44
Destin	Discerner and Virtuous	72
Destiny	Consecrated to God	58
Dexter	Diligent	70
Diana	God's Glory	66
Diane	God's Glory	66
Dohn	God's Gift	100
Dominique	Belonging	58
Donald - Don	Overcomer	174
Donika	Strength of Character	162
Donna	Dignity of Character	162
Dora	Gift of God	94
Dorain	Devoted Heart	66
Dorcus	Graceful	104
Doreen	Devoted Heart	66
Doris	Excellent Virtue	88

Index

Name	Character	Page
Dorothy - Dorthea	Gift of God	94
Douglas	Seeker of Light	158
Drake	Courageous Spirit	46
Drew	Strong Manly	164
Duane	Cheerful	154
Duncan	Loyal One	118
Dustin	Loyal One	118
Dwight	Dweller in Truth	158
Earl	Man of Honor	122
Earlene	Youthful One	168
Earnest	Devoted One	66
Edgar	Courageous	134
Edith	God's Gift	100
Edmond - Edmund	Prosperous Protector	142
Edna	Prosperous Protector	142
Edward	Prosperous Protector	142
Edwin	Guardian	142
Eileen	Light	160
Elaine - Elayne	Bright One	150
Elbert	Man of God	64
Eldon	Bright One	150
Eleanor	Bright One	150
Eli	God's Honor	122
Elijha	Bright One	42
Elisa	Consecrated	58
Elise	Consecrated	58
Elizabeth	Consecrated	58
Ella	Bright One	160
Ellen	Bright One	150
Ellery	Noble One	110
Ellie	Light	160
Elouise	Bright One	110
Elroy	Excellent Worth	80
Elsa - Elsja	Consecrated One	58

Index

Name	Character	Page
Elsie	Consecrated One	58
Emily	Diligent	70
Emma	Caring One	48
Erica - Erika	Woman of Esteem	78
Erick - Erik	Godly Power	120
Erin - Eran	Peaceful Friend	38
Ernest	Devoted	66
Ervin	Friendly	38
Erwin	Friendly	38
Essie	Humble	64
Esther	Humble	48
Ethan	Steadfast	74
Ethel	Dignity of Character	162
Eugene	Born Noble	118
Eunice	Joy with Victory	160
Eva	Full of Life	52
Evan	God's Gift	100
Eve	Full of Life	52
Evelyn	Light	150
Evirette	Mighty One	134
Ezekiel	Bright One	150
Ezra	Noble Spirit	124
Fara	Beauty	106
Farley	Beauty	106
Farrah	Beauty	106
Faye - Fay	Faith	82
Felix - Felex	Fortunate	92
Fergus	Steadfast	62
Fernard	Life Adventure	168
Flora	Sower of Cheer	52
Florence	Sower of Cheer	52
Floyd	Wise One	180
Forrest	Strong Manly	164
Frances - Francis	Living in Freedom	156

Index

Name	Character	Page
Frank	Living in Freedom	15
Franklin	Freeman	15
Fred	Peaceful	7
Freda	Peaceful	12
Fredrick	Peaceful	7
Fushia	Bringer of Truth	17
Gabriel - Gabrial	Man of God	6
Gail-Gale-Gayle	Source of Joy	5
Galen	One who Heal	8
Garrett	Courageous	17
Gary	Loyalty	11
Gay - Gaye	A Merry Heart	5
Gaylen	Joyful One	5
Gene	Born Noble	11
Genevieve - Genevive	Pure	13
George	Industrious	9
Georgene - Georgine	Industrious	9
Georgette	Caring One	4
Georgia	Industrious	9
Gerald - Ged	God's Warrior	17
Geraldine	Appointed by God	4
Gerard	Loyal Heart	11
Gerold	Loyal Heart	11
Gerrit	Brave	4
Gertrude	Courageous	12
Gideon	God's Warrior	17
Gilbert	Noble Spirit	12
Giles	Loyal Heart	11
Gillian	Youthful	15
Gina	Humble Spirit	4
Ginger	Pure One	13
Gladys	God's Princess	10
Glecy	Princess	10
Glenda - Glennda	Increasing Faith	8

Index

Name	Character	Page
Glen - Glenn	Prosperous One	92
Glori	Glory to God	36
Gloria	Glory to God	36
Gedieon - Gedion	Warrior	180
Gene	Born Noble	118
Gordon	Asending One	120
Grace	Thankful Spirit	48
Grant	Generous One	88
Gratton	Generous	90
Greg	Watchful	88
Gregory	Watchful	88
Gretchen	Pure One	132
Griffin	Man of Distinction	162
Gunda	Mighty Warrior	178
Gunner	Mighty Warrior	178
Gus	Industrious	92
Guy	Watchful	88
Gwendolyn	Blessed One	108
Hal	Strong Leader	134
Haley	Powerful	134
Hank	Strong Leader	46
Hannah	Full of Grace	104
Harlan	Strong Leader	134
Harley	Strong Leader	134
Harold	Powerful	134
Harriet	Full of Wisdom	180
Harry	Strong Leader	46
Harvey	Loyal	118
Hazel	Quiet Spirit	148
Heather	Joyful Spirit	52
Hector	Steadfast	62
Heidi	Full of Honor	122
Helen	Bright One	150
Hennritta	Industrious	92

18

Index

Name	Character	Page
Henry	Industrious	9
Herbert	Diligent Workers	7
Herman	Man of Loyalty	11
Hester	Guardian	14
Hilda	Woman of Strength	16
Holly	Pure	14
Honore	Esteemed One	7
Hope	Trustful	17
Horace	Loyal and Brave	11
Hover	Loyal and Brave	11
Howard	Reasonable	7
Hubert	Man of Honor	12
Hugh	Man of Reason	6
Humphery	Peaceful Spirit	7
Ida	Joyful One	10
Ilene	Joyful One	10
Imogene	God's Grace	10
Inez	Inner Beauty	10
Ingrid	Inner Beauty	10
Iona	Living Fragrance	5
Ira	Living Fragrance	15
Irene	Peaceful Spirit	12
Iris	God's Promise	4
Irvin	Manly	16
Irving	Faithful Friend	3
Irwin	Friendly One	3
Isaac - Issac	God is my Helper	6
Isabel	Consecrated	5
Isaiah	God's Gracious Gift	6
Iva	God's Gracious Gift	14
Ivan	God's Gracious Gift	14
Iverna	Declarer of God	14
Jack	Truthful	17
Jacqueline	Truthful	17
Jacob	Truthful	17

Index

Name	Character	Page
Jake	Truthful	172
James	Truthful	172
Jamie	Truthful	172
Jan	God's Gift	94
Jana	God's Gift	94
Jane - Janie	Gracious	104
Janelle - Janelle	God's Gracious	94
Janet	God's Gracious Gift	94
Janice	God's Gracious Gift	94
Jasmine	Refreshing	154
Jason	One who Heals	88
Jay	Integrity	122
Jean - Jeanie - Jeni	Wisdom	180
Jeanette	God's Gracious Gift	180
Jed	Discerning Spirit	72
Jeffery - Jeffrey	Peaceful	74
Jeneva	Esteemed	78
Jenifer - Jennifer	Fair Lady	104
Jeremiah	Appointed by God	40
Jeremy	Appointed by God	40
Jerald - Jerold	Appointed by God	40
Jerome	Devoted Heart	66
Jerrelle - Jerrile	Appointed by God	40
Jerry	Appointed by God	40
Jerusha	Beautiful	106
Jesse	God Exists	82
Jessica - Jessie	Blessed One	82
Jewel	Precious One	136
Jill	Young Heart	168
Jim - Jimmy	Truthful	172
Jo	Increasing Youth	82
Joan - Joane	Gift of God	94
Jody	Praised by God	80

Index

Name	Character	Page
Joel	Declare of God	148
Johan - Johnnan	God's Precious Gift	100
Johanna	God's Precious Gift	100
John	God's Precious Gift	100
Jolene - Joline	Faith Toward God	82
Jonas	Peaceful	78
Jonathan	God's Precious Gift	100
Jonette - Jonnette	God's Precious Gift	100
Joni	God's Precious Gift	100
Jordan	Full of Joy	54
Joseph	Increasing Faith	82
Josephine	Increasing Faith	82
Joshua	God is Savior	156
Joy	Joyful	108
Joyce	Joyful	108
Juan	God's Gracious Gift	100
Juanita	God's Gracious Gift	100
Judith	Praised by God	82
Judson	Praised by God	82
Judy	Praised by God	82
Julia - Jilie - Jule	Youthful One	168
Jullian - Julian	Youthful One	168
Julianna	Youthful One	168
Juliet	Youthful One	168
Julius	Youthful One	168
June	Benevolent Heart	46
Justin	Just One	62
Kari - Karrie	Strong Womanly	106
Karl	Strong Manly	164
Karen - Karin	Pure One	146
Karla	Strong Womanly	164
Kathy - Cathy	Pure One	146
Katherine - Katheryn	Pure One	146
Katie - Katy	Pure One	146

Index

Name	Character	Page
Kay	Pure One	146
Keith	Secure One	156
Kelly - Kelley	Excellent Virtue	104
Kelvin	Humble	116
Kendall	Priceless and Strong	138
Kendra	The Knowing Woman	72
Keneth - Kenneth	Gracious Manly	164
Kent	Priceless and a Light	138
Kenton	Dependent on God	64
Kerry	Seeker of Light	136
Keturah - Ketura	Precious	136
Kevin	Kind One	116
Kimball	Strong Enduring	164-166
Kimberly	Noble One	166
Kirby	Worshipful Spirit	36
Kirt - Kurt	A Counselor	44
Krista - Crista	Follower of Christ	86
Kristal - Cristal	Follower of Christ	86
Kristen - Cristin	Follower of Christ	86
Kristy - Kristie	Follower of Christ	86
Kyle	Integrity	72
Lacy - Lacie	Cheerful	154
Lama	Diligent	70
Lamar	Diligent	70
Lana	Fair Countenance	104
Lance	God's Warrior	178
Larita	A Pearl	136
Lark	A Merry Heart	154
Larry	Victorious	174
Latoya	Victorious	174
Laura - Lora	Victorious	174
Laurel	Victorious	174
Lauren	Victorious	174
Loretta - Laurette	Victorious	174

Index

Name	Character	Page
Laurie - Lori	Victorious	174
Lavelle - Lavel	Purity	146
Laverne	Pure One	132
Lavina	Purity	146
Lavonne	Abundant Life	174
Lawen	Victorious	176
Lawence	Victorious	176
Leah - Lee - Leigh	Contented One	128
Leann - Leanne	Contented One	128
Lenore	Bright One	156
Leona	Woman of Courage	48
Leonard	Courageous	46
Leon - Leone	Brave	46
Leorurita	Victorious	176
Leroy	Excellent Worth	84
Lesley - Leslie	Calm Spirit	124
Lewis - Louis	Victorious	176
Lexie - Lexey	Truthful	173
Lila	Light	46
Lillian	Pure Heart	162
Lilly	A Light	16
Lincoln	Refreshing One	154
Linda	Beauty	106
Linsay	Refreshing One	154
Lisa	Consecrated	54
Loyld - Lloyd - Lolyd	Wise	74
Lois	Victorious	11
Lola	Compassion	8
Lomo	Tender Hearted	9
Loraine	Victorious	174
Loren	Victorious	174
Lotta	Diligent	74
Lorenza	Victorious	174
Lorenzo	Victorious	176

Index

Name	Character	Page
Louise - Loes	Victorious	112
Lourdes	Gracious	104
Lowell	Beloved One	44
Luann - Luanne	Victorious	174
Lucile	Bringer of Light	160
Lucy - Luci	Bringer of Light	160
Luke	Enlightened One	150
Luther	Victorious	176
Lycinda - Cindy	Bringer of Light	150
Lydia	Worshiper of God	36
Lyle	Sojourner	58
Lyndon	Refreshing One	154
Lynn	Refreshing One	52
Mabel - Mable	Loving Heart	48
Mac	Transformed Heart	168
Madeline	Transformed Heart	168
Magdalena	Exalted One	78
Maggie	Pearl	132
Malcolm - Mal	Teachable Spirit	72
Mandy	Beloved	44
Manfred	Faithful Friend	38
Manuel	God is With Us	62
Maranda	Generous Heart	90
Mercedes	Brave Heart	46
Marcella	Brave Heart	48
Marcelle	Great One	120
Marcia	Brave Heart	47
Marcus - Marcos	Mighty Warrior	178
Margaret-Margarette	Pearl	132
Margrita - Margritte	Pearl	132
Margo	Pearl	132
Margot	Pearl	132
Maria	Living Fragrance	52
Mariam - Marian	Expression of Worship	36
Marie	Living Fragrance	52

Index

Name	Character	Page
Marilyn	Pearl	132
Marion	Living Fragrance	52
Marissa	Lady of Victory	112
Marjorie - Marge	Pearl	132
Mark	Mighty Warrior	120
Marlea	Precious	130
Marlene	Living Fragrance	52
Marlin	Loyal	118
Marlisa	Pure One	132
Marlow - Marlowe	Gift of God	100
Marsha	Strength of Character	162
Marshall	Loyal	118
Martha	Woman of Distinction	146
Martin	Vigilant	120
Marvel	Joyous	54
Marvin - Marvine	Friendly One	38
Mary	Living Fragrance	52
Maryann - Marianne	Worship Spirit	36
Matthew	Gift of God	94
Maureen	God's Grace	102
Maurice	Courageous	40
Maxine	Esteemed	70
May - Mae	Esteemed	70
Maynard	Steadfast	62
Meagan	Strong Spirit	138
Mel	Precious	130
Melanie - Melanine	Courageous	40
Melba	Precious	130
Melinda	Gracious	104
Melissa	Pure One	140
Melody	Joyful	102
Melvin	Reliable	82
Meredith	Blessed by God	8
Merle	Generous	88

Index

Name	Character	Page
Merlin	Generous	88
Mervin	Friendly	38
Mia	Belongs to God	58
Micah	Godliness	66
Michael	Godliness	66
Michelle	Godliness	66
Mildred	Gentle One	90
Miles	Full of Mercy	88
Milton - Milt	Prosperous	92
Minnie	Effectionate	48
Miranda	Generous	90
Miriam	Living Fragrance	52
Missy	Generous	88
Misty	Generous	88
Mitchel - Mitchael	Godliness	66
Mitzie	Great in Forgiveness	88
Moe	Abiding with God	36
Molly	Living Fragrance	52
Monica	Woman of Wisdom	180
Monique	Full of Wisdom	180
Montgomery	Exalted	78
Morris	Sincere Devotion	66
Moses	Delivered by God	36
Muriel	Bright with Joy	160
Murray	Cheerful Spirit	154
Myra	Gentle	90
Myron	Strong Manly	164
Nadine	Hopeful	44
Nancy	Gracious One	104
Nanette	Full of Grace	104
Natalie	Joyous One	108
Natasha	Gift of God	100
Nathan	Given of God	94
Nathanael-Nathaniel	Given of God	94

Index

Name	Character	Page
Neal - Neil	Champion	8
Nel	Champion	11
Nelson	Champion	8
Newman	Transformed	16
Nicholas	Victorious	17
Nicole	Victorious	17
Noah	Comforter	3
Noble	Man of Honor	12
Noel	Joyful	10
Noma	Precious	13
Nora - Norah	Honorable	12
Noreen - Noriene	Honorable	12
Norma	Godliness	12
Norman	Mighty	12
Odel	Peaceful	6
Olive	Peaceful	12
Oliver	Peaceful	7
Olivia	Peaceful	12
Oloph - Olaph	Peaceful	6
Omega	Gift of God	10
Orin	Steadfast Endurance	6
Orpha - Oprah	Gift of God	10
Oscar	Blessed in Service	8
Oswald	In God's Strength	6
Otha	Gift of God	10
Otis	Gift of God	10
Owen	Youthful	15
Paige	Obedient	12
Pamela	Sweet Spirit	14
Patricia - Tricia	Honorable	12
Patrick	Honorable	12
Paul	Dependent on God	6
Paula	Follower of God	17
Pauline	Dependent of God	17

27

Index

Name	Character	Page
Pearl - Pearle	Pure Heart	146
Peggy	Precious One	136
Penny	Creative	148
Percy	Seeker of Wisdom	136
Perry	Strong Spirit	178
Peter	Strong Spirit	178
Philip	Strong Spirit	178
Philomena	Enlightened One	150
Phoebe	Wise One	180
Phylis - Phyllis	Tender Hearted	88
Polly	Living Fragrance	52
Priscilla	Wisdom	180
Queen - Quinta	Devoted	62
Quintin - Quinn	Manly	80
Rachael - Rachel	Little Lamb	170
Rae	Little Lamb	170
Rain - Raine	Mighty	120
Ralph	Manly	80
Ramona	Strong in Virtue	124
Ranata - Renata	Born Anew	36
Randal - Randall	Loyal	118
Randolph - Randoph	Loyal	118
Raymond	Loyal	134
Raynor	Mighty	122
Reba	Devoted	66
Rebecca - Rebkah	Devoted	66
Reed	Courageous	46
Regina	Gift of God	94
Reginald	Courageous	178
Renee - Renae	Born Anew	36
Reuben-Rueben-Ruben	Gift of God	100
Rex	Man of Authority	96
Reynold	Mighty	120
Rhea	Mighty	120

Index

Name	Character	Page
Rhoda	Fragrant Spirit	162
Rhonda	Strength of Character	162
Richard	Brave	46
Rick - Ricky	Brave	46
Rita	Pearl	136
Roan-Roanne-Roanna	Inner Beauty	106
Robert - Bob - Bobby	Excellent Worth	80
Roberta	Excellent Worth	80
Robin	Strength of Character	162
Robinson	Shining with Fame	150
Rochelle	Little Lamb	170
Rocky	Transformed Heart	168
Rodger - Roger	God's Warrior	178
Rodney	Esteemed One	134
Roena	Born Anew	78
Roind	Adored	78
Roland	Manly	80
Roman	Brave and Noble	46
Ronald	Mighty Powerful	120
Rose - Rosa	Giver of Love	116
Roseline - Rosene	Giver of Love	116
Ross	Gallant	178
Rowe	Esteemed	78
Rowen	Excellent Worth	80
Rowena	Esteemed	78
Roxanne - Roxann	Bright One	150
Ruby	Pure One	146
Rudolph	Loyal	118
Russsell - Russel	Wise Discretion	90
Ruth	Compassionate	90
Ryan	Champion	176
Sabrina	Woman of God	170
Saciko	A Friend	38
Sadie	Pure	102

Index

Name	Character	Page
Sally	God's Princess	102
Salvador	In God's Image	66
Samantha	Teachable One	72
Samuel	Integrity	122
Sandra	Inner Beauty	106
Sarah - Sara	Princess	102
Sarena	Princess	102
Scott	Loyal	118
Sean	God's Gift	100
Selina - Selena	Reflection of Light	150
Selma-Selmer-Selmar	Strong in Faith	82
Seth	Chosen of God	40
Shane	God's Gracious Gift	100
Shannon	Gracious Spirit	148
Sharlene	Strength of Character	162
Sharon	Princess	102
Shavona - Shavone	Princess	102
Shawn	Princess	100
Shelby	Dwells with God	36
Shella - Shellia	Contented Heart	170
Shelly - Shelley	Protector of Life	142
Sherman	Industrious	92
Sheri - Sherry	Cherished One	136
Sheryl	Peaceful	128
Shirley	Restful Spirit	128
Sidney	Excellent Discerner	72
Silas	Depth of Wisdom	180
Silvia - Sylvia	Secure One	156
Simon - Simeon	Obedient Spirit	124
Skip - Skipper	Warrior	178
Sondra	Inner Beauty	106
Sonia - Sonya	Wise Spirit	180
Sophia	Full of Wisdom	180
Spencer	Faithful Steward	168

Index

Name	Character	Page
Stacy - Stacey	Transformed Heart	168
Stasha	Victorious	112
Stella	Woman of Esteem	78
Stephan - Stephon	Crowned One	62
Stephanie	Crowned One	62
Stephen-Steven-Steve	Crowned One	62
Sterling	Excellent Character	80
Steward - Stewert	Helpful Spirit	88
Sue	Pure in Grace	58
Susan - Susie	Pure in Grace	58
Susana	Pure in Grace	58
Susane - Suzanne	Pure in Grace	58
Sybil	Freedom	156
Sylvester	Gift of God	94
Tabatha	Strong Womanly	166
Tamara - Tamera	Seeker of Truth	158
Tamela - Tammy	Sweet Spirit	108
Tandi - Tandy	Seeking One	158
Tania - Tonya	Noble Spirit	122
Tara	Exalted One	78
Tava	Exalted One	78
Taylor	Industrious One	92
Ted	Protector	142
Tedmund	Protector	142
Terah	Exalted One	78
Terence - Terrence	Man of Virtue	72
Teresa - Theresa	Industrious	92
Teva	Noble	122
Thaddeous	Giver of Praise	36
Thaddeus	Giver of Praise	36
Thelma	Trustful Heart	170
Theodore	Gift of God	94
Thomas-Tom-Tommy	Seeker of Truth	158
Tiffanie - Tiffany	In God's Image	78
Timothy	Honoring God	64

Index

Name	Character	Page
Tina	Obedient	124
Tineka - Tinica	Obedient	124
Toby	God's Goodness	64
Tracy	Industrious One	92
Trent	Persevering	64
Trevor	Prudent	124
Todd	Industrious	92
Troy	Mighty Powerful	120
Trudy - Trudi	Courageous	120
Truman	Faithful	82
Tyler	Industrious	92
Tyron - Tyrone	Esteemed One	78
Uretha - Uritha	Morning Light	52
Valeria	Steadfast	70
Valorie	Determined Purpose	70
Vance	Victorious	176
Vera	Faithful Spirit	70
Verlin	Increasing Faith	82
Verna	Full of Faith	82
Vernon	Abundant Life	92
Veronica	True Hearted	38
Verrie - Varrie	Faithful	82
Vickie	Victorious	174
Victor	Victorious	176
Victoria	Victorious	174
Vincent - Vince	Victorious	134
Viola	Humble	46
Violet	Humble	46
Virgil	Strong Bold	74
Virginia	Pure One	146
Vivian	Full of Light	52
Vonette	Born Anew	36
Wade	Champion	176
Waggner - Waggoner	Creative Spirit	72

Index

Name	Character	Page
Wallace - Wally	Industrious	92
Walter	Powerful	134
Wanda	Walks with God	36
Warner	Protector	142
Warren	Protector	142
Wayne	Lifter of Cares	64
Webster	Industrious	92
Weeks	Noble	122
Wendall - Wendel	Walks with God	36
Wendy - Wendi	Walks with God	170
Wesley	Prosperous	92
Whitman	Man of Reason	72
Whitney	Seeker of Wisdom	158
Wilber - Wilbur	Honorable	122
Willard	Diligent	70
Wilford - Willford	Peacemaker	74
Willfred - Wilfred	Peacemaker	74
William - Bill - Billy	Great Protector	142
Willie Mae	Protecter	142
Wilma	Giver of Security	142
Winifred	Pure	96
Winnie	Pure	96
Woodrow	Gift of God	94
Woodwill	Gift of God	94
Wynona	Belongs to God	58
Yvonne	Courageous	120
Zachariah-Zechariah	The Lord Remembers	148
Zachary	The Lord Remembers	148
Zaldy	Powerful	134
Zelda	Mighty	134
Zelfred	Bringer of Peace	74
Zelma	Devinely	156
Zenobia	Princess	102
Zepy	Obedient	124

Index

Name	Character	Page
Zoe	Life	154
Zola	Gracious	38
Zona	Steadfast	62
Zora	Morning Light	52
Zsa Zsa	Purity	58

Abiding To Dwell And Worship

Beth
Bethany
Glori
Gloria
Kirby
Lydia
Mariam
Marian
Maryann
Marianne
Moe
Moses
Ranata
Renee
Renae
Shelby
Thaddeus
Thaddeous
Vonnette
Wanda
Wendall
Wendel

Abiding With God   *Worshipful Spirit*

Patience and obedience are your lessons best learned,
Complete with each trial to guide away from being spurned.
Now the road is straight and narrow, as you obediently found out,
For that's the beauty you show forth in your victoriously loud shout.
Hallelujah! Hallelujah! Angels sing a song with you.
Because they know what you can do.
Happy are the words you sing, A mountain shall move this day for you.
Hallelujah! Hallelujah! is your shout of victory.
A plan complete is turning now all life to victory.
Holy is the Lord, as you kneel at His feet.
He touches you so you can see His highest love for thee.
Holy, Holy is the Lord and Holy He wants you to be,
All knowing of the Father, His grace poured out for thee.

A Friend With Peace

Alvin
Connie
Constance
Ervin
Erin
Erwin
Irving
Irwin
Manfred
Marvin
Marvine
Mervin
Noah
Saciko
Veronica

A Friend

Have you looked at you today?
Do you see what I can see?
Your kindness warmed a heart,
And your laughter tickled me.
You are eager to get up and go,
Just where the wind might blow.
Did you think I did not know
That some of you is show?
Those tears you hold inside. Weep, weep.
It heals the inner place you let not others peep.
Often a moment wasted is a day gained for you;
When you took time to hug a loved one,
It became a full day for you.
To know you is to see life in all its seasons,
Winter, Summer, Fall and Spring.
Winter stands for the lonely times;
Summer brings life's trials;
Fall coming to drop away your cares;
Spring to show forth the repairs.
I'm glad you are my friend, a lifetime of reasons,
I can call on you whatever the season.

Appointed By God

Adam
Alpha
Artis
Geraldine
Iris
Jeremiah
Jeremy
Jerrell
Jerrelle
Jerrille
Jerold
Jerry
Rueben
Ruben
Seth
Ziola

Appointed By God

A purpose and plan for you, appointed by God,
As you come to the Savior and walk upon His sod.
You shall be a light in the darkness, used for God's glory,
To show forth His love and tell the great story.
The story of Jesus and how He died for us all,
His love so deep, to forgive sin, big and small.
Nothing more can He do to prove His love for you;
He hasn't forgotten His plan that He has for you.
God is waiting and watching, and teaching His love;
You'll see the vision of Jesus, coming from above.
To gather his believers, His very own bride;
No more the saints be scattered, but on the clouds will ride.
For time is getting short and the story must be told to all,
That's His purpose and plan for you have heard His call.
Rise up and be ready, with God's love in your heart,
For God is the potter and the clay is your part.
A vessel you'll be for you heard the Father's cry,
And you will see Jesus when He splits the eastern sky.
To bring home His own, away from all stress,
And keep you in His presence, in His arms you'll rest.

The Church His Bride

Revelation 21:9,11
"And there came unto me one of the seven angels which had the seven vials full of seven of the last plagues, and talked with me, saying 'Come hither, I will show thee the bride, the Lamb's wife."

". . . having the glory of God and her light wa like unto a stone most precious even like a jasper stone, clear as crystal.'"

Ephesians 5:27
That He might present it to Himself a glorious church not having spot or wrinkle or any such thing but that it should be Holy and without blemish.

"The Church Is The Bride Of Christ"

Ephesians 5:27

Present Yourselves Holy and Without Blemish

Beloved

Alfred
Amanda
Amy
Avery
Darla
Darlene
Darrell
Darryl
David
Desirae
Desiree
Gina
Kirt
Kurt
Lowell
Nadine
Mandy

Beloved

You are called beloved, and that is a big word,
For God looks on the heart, not the outer nerd.
A pure heart you have, has been brought to attention,
And favor for you, I must not forget to mention.
You are loved because of your mercy, my friend,
Not judging others for the deeds they lend.
You are respected and people will listen to you,
Advice you give can comfort, a mood so blue.
Stay humble and you will not lose respect,
You see, friends rely on you, can you detect?
Sometimes you think what is life all about.
Just keep your chin up and remember not to pout.
There is a plan, your life will not be hollow,
Seek ye first the Kingdom of God, all else will follow.
Your closest friend will be the Son of God,
Jesus is His name, you'll learn, walking this sod.
Great is the Lord and greatly to be praised,
For it was His life He gave so we might be raised.
He had a heart full of love to forgive and save,
So you could be free, and for you His life He gave.

Brave Humble Leader

Aubrey
Arnold
Boyd
Caleb
Dean
Drake
Gerrit
Hank
Harry
Hover
Leon
Leone
Leonard
Lila
Marcedes
Maurice
Reed
Richard
Rick
Ricky
Roman
Viola
Violet

Humble Brave Leader

Humble are your words each day,
The action of your heart, display.
Although your heart is humble and contrite,
Being brave has not left your sight.
Brave as the highest in rank,
You go about your life as though driving a tank.
Life gets complicated, but problems do cease,
For you drive on, knowing the source of release.
Bravery has no fear, for it is bold,
It cannot be measured in weights of gold.
Standing up for what you believe,
Making sure the enemy will not deceive.
Looking first to God, to whom you will thank,
Then blessings will come from the heavenly bank.
People do need to hear God's word,
He can count on you to share and observe.
For you are brave, the truth to speak,
And casting all to those, salvation seek,
Jesus our Savior, we are told,
Face to face, we shall behold.

Brave Loving Heart

Billie Jean
Catrisse
Charity
Claude
Claudette
Claudia
Emma
Esther
Georgette
Grace
June
Leona
Mabel
Mable
Marcella
Marcia
Melanie
Melanine
Minnie

Brave Loving Heart

Brave little lady, you have a loving heart,
Did you ever wonder just what is your part?
A full life we live in this world we occupy,
Your words mean much, there is no time to be shy.
Use your heart to tell what's on your mind,
And speak the situations, the answers will entwine.
Why do you hide the real you inside?
Express yourself, inside of you God does reside.
Aren't you glad He gave you a loving heart?
For it is only today that we can do our part.
Oh, at times it seems that you do gripe,
But that's okay, if your tears, you let Him wipe.
We don't have to be perfect, only honest and true,
You'll see it brings satisfaction where action is due.
Sometimes the struggles of life, you'll have to fight,
Hang on to your knowledge with all of your might.
Why do yo think you are not worthy of God's love?
He paid the price and His mercy endures above.
Relax and know, for you He gave His son,
You are His child, and in Him we are all "one".
One day Jesus our Lord will come to be our Host,
To take us home, glory to the Father, Son and
   Holy Ghost.

Sermon On The Mount

Matthew 5:2-16

And He opened His mouth and taught them saying: Blessed are the poor in spirit for theirs is the Kingdom of heaven. Blessed are they that mourn, for they shall be comforted. Blessed are the meek for they shall inherit the earth. Blessed are they who hunger and thirst after righteousness for they shall be filled. Blessed are the merciful for they shall receive mercy. Blessed are the peacemakers for they shall be called children of God. Blessed are they who are persecuted for righteousness sake, for theirs is the Kingdom of heaven. Blessed are you when men revile you and persecute you, for they did persecute the prophets which were before you.

Ye are the salt of the earth, but if the salt loses its savior, where shall it be salted? It is good for nothing, but to be cast out, and to be trodden under foot of men.

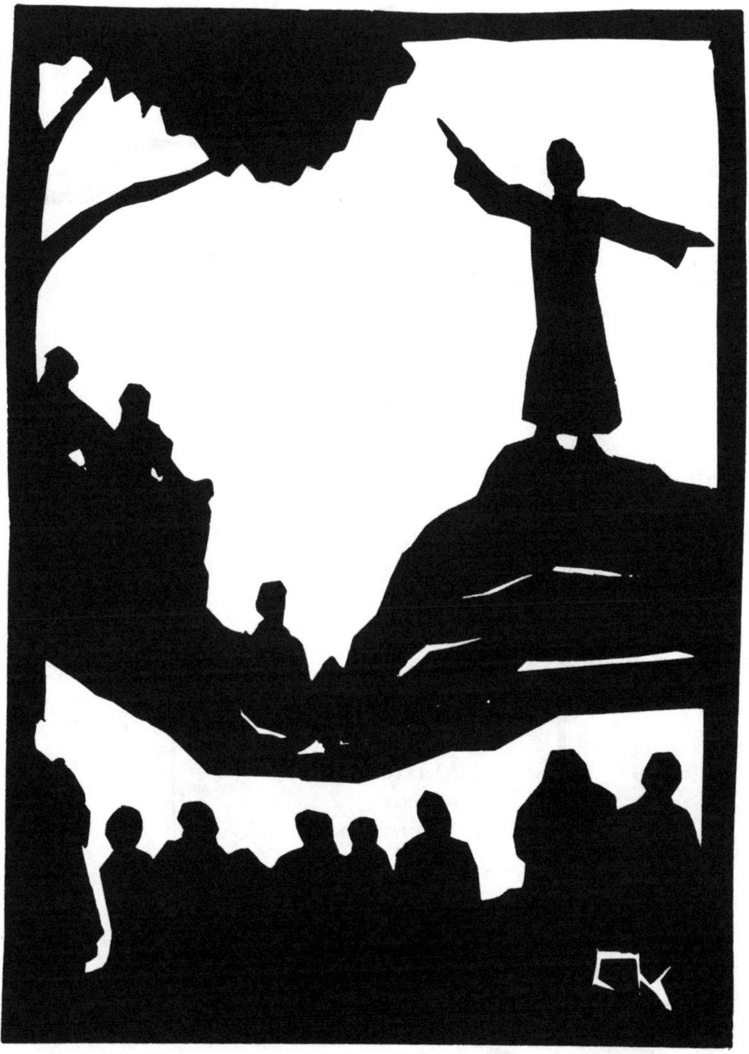

Cheerful Fragrance of Life

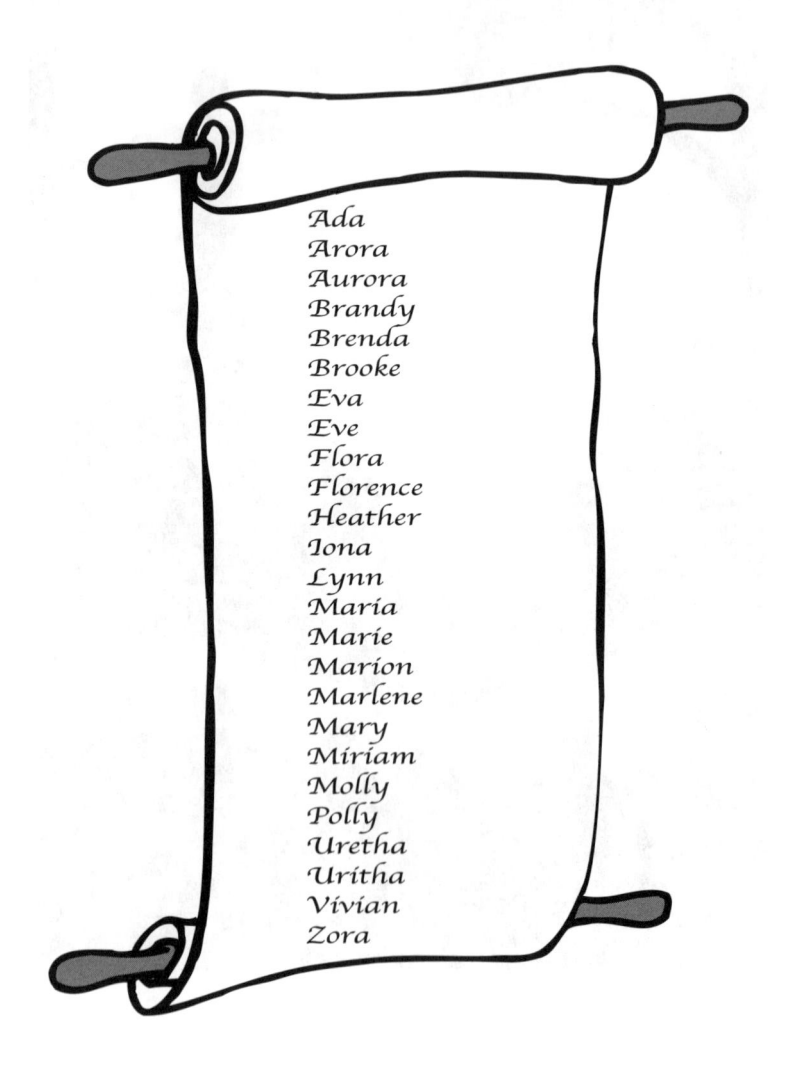

Ada
Arora
Aurora
Brandy
Brenda
Brooke
Eva
Eve
Flora
Florence
Heather
Iona
Lynn
Maria
Marie
Marion
Marlene
Mary
Miriam
Molly
Polly
Uretha
Uritha
Vivian
Zora

Cheerful Living Fragrance

Much like flowers, you flourish and stand in beauty,
As the flower seed is planted to fill its duty.
So it is with you, you grow, you mature,
To the fullness you were created to be.
Your cheerfulness spreads to those around,
While your joyful giggle pleases beyond its sound.
Patience tells me you are willing to wait for the very best,
Even to suffer, you pass the test.
God calls you His child and each tear He will understand,
Who can separate His love, it's like a wedding band.
Same as the "lily of the valley" blowing in the wind,
You are strong to stand tall, against the world's sin.
It's good to know someone like you,
The way you share and care for others, too.
Your beauty is rare and seen in the eyes of love,
From our Father up above.

Bringer of Joy

Babs
Barbara
Barbel
Barble
Bea
Beata
Beatrice
Bennett
Dawn
Gail
Gayle
Gay
Gaylen
Joran
Marvel

Bringer of Joy

Coming with joy for all to see,
A contagious reaction from you to me.
Joy is what the world does need,
A strength for us, within this seed.
Uplifting the heart, to bring a smile,
And your mouth, there is no guile.
It's easy to laugh when there is joy,
Much like the life of a little boy.
Bundled inside is a heart's reply,
This joy expose and don't deny.
Joy unexpressed is as buried in the sand,
Released, it will spread throughout the land.
Joy to the world, the Lord has come,
The Savior's love it's not just for some.
It's for all who hear and only receive,
A joy is born, when we can believe.
So share your joy and let it explode,
Because you are received within his abode.
Joy to the world, the Lord has come, you see
A contagious reaction from you to me.

Deliverance

Luke 4:18

"The spirit of the lord is upon me, because he hath appointed me to preach to the poor; he hath sent me to heal the broken hearted; to preach deliverance to the captives, and recovering of sight to the blind, to set at liberty them that are bruised."

Peace

James 3:17,18

But the wisdom that is from above is first pure, then peaceable, gentle and easy to be entreated, full of mercy and good fruits without partiality and without hypocrisy. The fruit of righteousness is sown in peace of them that make peace.

Psalm 119:165

Great peace have they which love Thy law and nothing shall offend them.

Consecrated To God With Grace

Ava
Augustine
Bessie
Betsy
Betty
Charlotte
Destiny
Dominique
Elisa
Elise
Elsa
Elsja
Elsie
Elizabeth
Isabel
Lisa
Lyle
Mia
Sue
Susan
Susie
Susana
Suzanne
Wynona
Zsa-Zsa

Pure In Grace   Consecrated

You were set apart to be holy, I bet you didn't know,
Your path in life is not to go just anywhere the wind might blow.
But you are set apart by God, for His purpose and plan,
One day He'll call you and expect you to take a stand.
Will you submit to His loving kindness so true,
Or will you deny His life planned out for you.
You have a desire to travel the world over,
With your personality as rare as a four leaf clover.
You have a giving heart, but usually have no money to give.
Money isn't everything, people need more as they daily live.
So give what you have-love, encouragement and your time to care.
These are things, people really need to share.
After you have drank fresh water from God's fountain
Then you will be able to climb each and every mountain.
Yes, your personality is rare, you think you need no direction,
But you will learn to ask for guidance for your best protection.
Life is hard sometimes, impossible to remove the kink.
But the love you show will be the missing link.
Love breaks down the walls of bitterness, hate and strife
Then you will be able to get on the right pathway of life.
So fill your heart with mercy, forgiveness and love,
And continue to seek guidance from the Father above.

Our Commission

Mark 16:15-18

"Go ye into all the world, and preach the gospel to every creature. He that believeth and is baptized shall be saved; but he that believeth not shall be saved.

And these signs shall follow them that believe; In my name they shall cast out devils; they shall speak with new tongue;

They shall take up deadly serpents; and if they drink any deadly thing, it shall not hurt them, they shall lay hands on the sick and they shall recover."

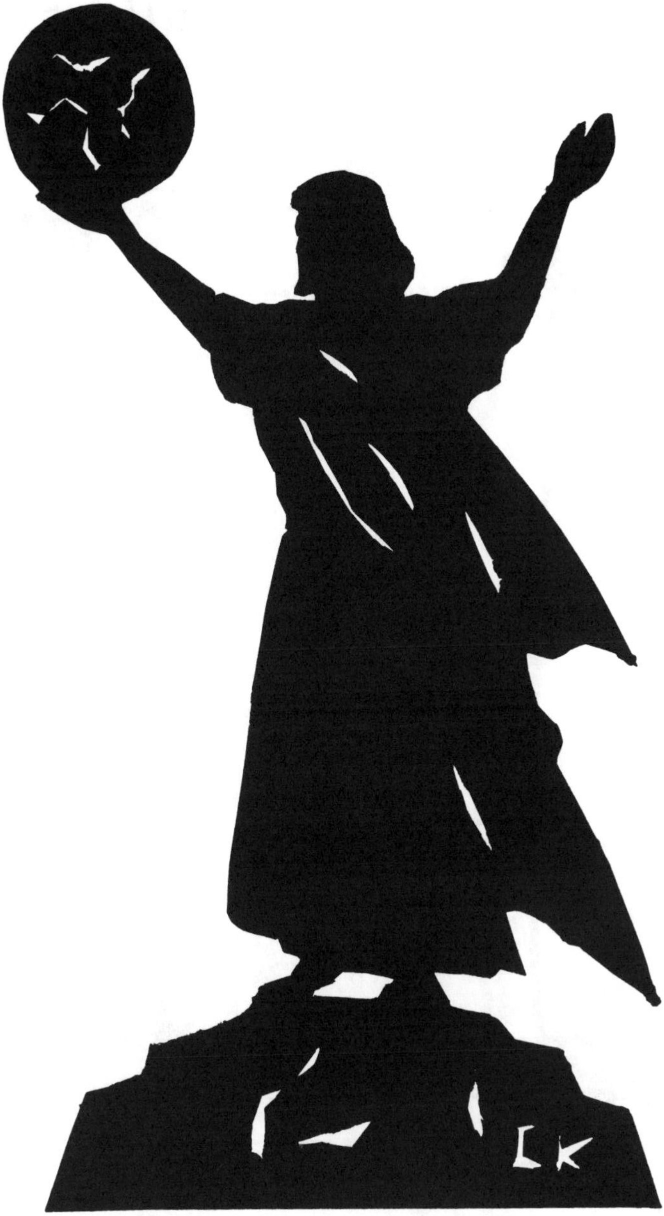

Crowned and Steadfast

Clyde
Currie
Curry
Curtis
Darcy
Fergus
Hector
Hugh
Justin
Manuel
Maynard
Orin
Queen
Quinta
Stephan
Stephanie
Stephen
Stephon
Steve
Steven
Zona

Crowned One   Steadfast

Steadfast you are to what you believe;
That's good and just, steadfast though naive.
Think on the things of right and wrong,
Then cast wrong down to become more strong.
It is great the way you study both sides before you judge,
Because if you didn't, I'm sure you would carry a grudge.
Thoughtful you are, steadfast and not deceived,
I know that it's God in who you believe.
In all your ways you try to be fair,
It's only your time to give to show you care.
Sensitive and strong are very good traits-
Use them wisely, remember reward is the "Pearly Gates".
In all of God's moments, He knows your thoughts,
And why He gave His only Son that you were bought.

Dependent On God

Abner
Blaine
Blaire
Blair
Carter
Elbert
Essie
Gabriel
Isaiah
Kenton
Odel
Olaph
Oloph
Oswald
Paul
Timothy
Toby
Trent
Wayne

Dependent On God

A man with a great big heart and little self-esteem,
Put them both together, it makes a tremendous team.
Your big heart reaches out, wherever it can,
And your little self-esteem keeps you a humble man.
It's satisfaction for you, depending on God for your source,
In all things be content, you will feel no remorse.
He sees you as a little child, looking to Him what is due,
Because you rely on Him and not what you can do.
God is big in your life and calls you His little man,
You know of His wisdom, He has counted each grain of sand.
God is mindful of all He has created and He really cares,
No wonder you rely on Him and are not afraid of snares.
Perfect peace go to them who put their trust in Him,
Yes, blessings are included, but your weakness He will trim.
For He sees you as you are, and is mindful of your needs,
He will bring you to a place of growing, just like a little seed.
You will grow and grow until your capacity is full grown,
All will know you are a child of God, by your love shown.
So rest in Him, your treasures are in heaven up above,
Learn all you can, to be ready with a perfect love.

Devoted Godliness

Adele
Adelle
Ardelle
Barnaby
Clayton
Daphine
Diana
Diane
Dorain
Doreen
Earnest
Ernest
Jerome
Micah
Michael
Michelle
Mitchel
Mitchael
Morris
Reba
Rebecca
Rebekah
Salvador

Devoted One

You are devoted to God and those in authority
Seeking righteousness in thought is your priority.
Always showing respect to your fellowman,
But raise up compassion, to lend a helping hand.
You need not try to be so reserved and mild
For you are precious in the sight of God, little child.
Strong, virtuous, full of joy is your stature,
So release your inner self, get ready for the rapture.
When Christ comes back to get his saints
You'll be in that number marching so quaint.
You seem to get depressed with the world we stay
Just keep your eyes on heaven, where your real treasures lay.
Don't let the worldly happenings, bring you down;
You are a conqueror, rise up with a happy sound.
Sing your songs of Jesus and play your music unto Him
Then you can count your blessings filled to the brim.
Yes, you are a child created by God.
He shall rule you by His love and not a rod.
And when He calls you to heaven's home,
You will see His riches in Glory, this world no more to roam.

Living Water

John 4:13-14

Jesus said unto her whosoever drinketh this water shall thirst again:

But whosoever drinketh this water that I shall give him shall never thirst;

But the water that I shall give them shall be in him a well of water springing up unto everlasting life.

Truth

Hebrews 4:12
For the word of God is quick and powerful and sharper than any two edge sword piercing even to divide asunder of soul and spirit and of the joints and marrow, and is a discerner of the thoughts and interests of the heart.

Psalm 119:89
Forever oh Lord your word is settled in heaven.

Revelation 21:7
"An he said unto me I am the Alpha and Omega; The beginning and the end. I will give to him that thirst of the fountain of water to life freely."

Diligent

Adrian
Amelia
April
Apryl
Barlett
Barlette
Beverly
Byron
Corbet
Corbit
Dexter
Emily
Herbert
Valorie
Valeria
Vera
Willard

Diligent Worker

A dreamer above all dreamers, who believes beyond all thoughts
That if you reach for a star, it shall be your star one day.
In all of God's creation you strive for the goal
As you begin to reach, reach up high,
Never ceasing, but sometimes pausing
For short glances of stillness all around.
Until the reaching starts again,
And your star will glow to all men.
You will go for the brightest, most precious star, pure and great,
And on it is written "Mighty Everlasting Faith."
There will be trouble of the sky,
Lightning and thunder, along with clashes of surrender.
But surrender you can not do!
So stretching on, you point your hand,
Till the clear skies come through.
And as you finally grab your star,
You'll receive the gift of faith in the palm of your hand,
And your eye shall behold all your dreams come true.

Discerner and Virtuous

Arthur
Brian-Brien
Cie
Cecil
Cecillia
Denise
Dennis
Destin
Howard
Jed
Kendra
Kyle
Loyld
Lolyd
Lloyd
Mal
Malcolm
Samantha
Sidney
Terence
Terrence
Waggner
Waggoner
Whitman

Descerning In Virtue

A discerner of the good and bad,
Can keep you satisfied from being sad.
Take time to watch and weigh things out,
So you will understand what life is all about.
It's not just to become famous and rich,
Open your eyes, less you fall into a ditch.
Your path in an eternal walk without end,
Praising the Savior, for wisdom He will send.
Learning and applying go together,
One is not good without the other.
Look to God each day, before it begins,
He will keep you from the world of sin.
You have always been the apple of God's eye,
For you are humble, and bow down to cry.
Jesus our Lord did walk these steps,
Your path to take, yes Jesus wept.
God sees you for your honesty, I say,
So keep your path straight, the narrow way.
Blessings will come to you, brought by the dove,
It is written He loves you, our Father of love.

Enduring With Peace

Craig
Ethan
Fred
Frederic
Humphrey
Jeffery
Jeffrey
Jonas
Oliver
Virgil
Willford
Wilford
Willfred
Wilfred
Zelfred

Enduring With Peace

You are a man of compassion and endurance to bring peace.
A sensitive touch for others is a gift that will not cease.
Because you are a peacemaker, you are called a child of God.
That is not to say that sometimes you would rather carry a rod.
Your long spans of time in thought are moments that cannot be bought.
For others could learn from you to take time and do as you do.
It is a special quality you've had that will bring you good instead of bad.
Always know that as you gaze,
Seek wisdom in all your ways.
They will know, you are weighing things out,
In the eyes of God, that is what it's all about.
Starting from birth, till death you will see,
It is God's pleasure for you to be.
The man of compassion and endurance, of peace for all to see.

Vision

Proverbs 29:18

Where there is no vision the people perish, but he that keepeth the law, happy is he.

Trust

Proverbs 3:5-6

Trust in the Lord with all thy heart and lean not to your own understanding. In all your ways acknowledge Him, and He shall direct thy path.

Esteemed One

Adeline
Adella
Darwin
Erica
Erika
Honore
Jeneva
Magdalena
Maxine
May
Mae
Montgomery
Roena
Roind
Rowe
Rowena
Samantha
Stella
Tara
Tava
Terah
Tiffanie
Tiffany
Tyron
Tyrone

Esteemed One

You are loved by God for your righteousness and loving the things that are true, right and just. A long view of righteousness is in the sight of your heart, separated by the wrong you see the world do. Don't be dismayed if others cannot see as you see, because one day, a clear picture will be their vision, too.

It's more important for you to act on righteousness in your own life, for that is how people learn and life becomes a living picture with love shining all around you.

Let mercy and forgiveness fill your heart to shun criticism, selfishness and judgement, then the picture of righteousness will be seen clearly in the eyes of others and in the eyes of God, our Father, who loves us all. He will be the final picture of righteousness. You are loved with the highest love for who you are, by our Creator, God.

Excellent Worth

Alvera
Elroy
Jody
Leroy
Neal
Neil
nelson
Quin
Quintin
Ralph
Robert
Bob
Bobby
Roberta
Roland
Rowen
Sterling

Excellent Worth

What is your worth you ask?
I can tell you, it is weighed by your task.
You can work hard each task you do,
Your worth is high, gains are done by you.
Still you feel you are worth little,
But remember I write not a riddle.
True words I say and for your sake
Be sure to know, your rewards no one can take.
Rest in each thing you do, it's for a reason,
Lest you might commit a treason.
A soldier in the Father's eyes, are you!
March for Him, conquer in what you do.
Carry the sword of truth by your side,
Then your righteousness you will not hide.
Your worth is more than you may see;
It's meant to live, all you should be.
For you are in the greatest army march,
Together with our Father, He shall watch.
So march on, you are worth more than precious things.
You are a soldier for the King of Kings.

Increasing Faith

Arlen
Arlene
Arleen
Benedict
Beulah
Fay
Faye
Glenda
Glennda
Jesse
Jessica
Jo
Jolene
Joline
Joseph
Josephine
Judith
Judy
Judson
Mel
Melvin
Meredith
Oscar
Selma
Selmar
Selmer
Truman
Verlin
Verna
Varrie
Verrie

Increasing Faith

Life is a long and busy road to hoe,
Don't let the little things bother you as you go.
Stand up and be counted, there is much to reap,
Don't be troubled, it is okay if you should weep.
An ever-increasing faithfulness have you,
And one day you will be called faithful and true.
Your life is something to laugh and sing about,
But a waste of time if you should put.
There is much for you to share with a friend,
Sometimes you will rely on advice they might lend.
Be faithful to each one you should meet,
A friend they may need and you will be in that seat.
A little time means a lot to someone in need,
And a helping hand is a friend indeed.
Are you looking forward to God's Kingdom above,
Where you shall see the completeness of real love?
Precious little lamb, as the Father sees you now,
You can call on Him when your head begins to bow.
God knows each heartache and each trial for sure,
He sees all your visions, to Him it is no blur.
For you have learned from each ache and pain,
And will come to understand it's not in vain.
You see, your faithfulness pleases God,
And with a smile, He does gently nod.

Faith

Hebrew 11:1; 11:33-34

Now the faith is the substance of things hoped for, the evidence of things not seen,

But without faith it is impossible to please God; he that cometh to God must believe that He is, and that He is a rewarder of them that seek Him.

Who through faith subdued Kingdoms, wrought righteousness, obtained promises, stopped the mouth of lions.

Matthew 17:17

O'faithless and perverse generation, how long shall I be with you? How long shall I suffer you? Bring him hither to me.

"According to your faith be it unto you"
Matthew 9:29

"Why are you fearful, oh ye of little faith"
Matthew 8:26

Follower of Christ

Chris
Christella
Christian
Kristian
Christina
Kristina
Christine
Kristine
Christoffer
Cristene
Krista
Crista
Kristal
Crystal
Kristen
Cristin
Kristy
Kristie

Follower of Christ

Sensible and practical are great traits you carry,
It will come in handy for the mate you marry.
Follower of Christ is what your name means,
Keep walking, the results shall manifest your dreams.
There are a lot of people who believe Jesus's words,
But few put them to action, it takes a lot of nerve.
Yes, some are saved by grace, and only sit and wait,
But you will join the march and gain your desired fate.
For you are not lazy and will rise to walk the path,
It will take endurance, yet keep you for the wrath.
To follow Christ is to follow after righteousness every day,
Ignoring each hindrance, not stopping along the way.
Your landmark is who you follow, for guidance and direction,
And thru the stormy weather, he will be there for your protection.
So walk on through the wind and rain, to be above the strife,
Some will be amazed to see all you accomplish in your life.
We only live once, here in this world, and for a short span,
So try to keep your eye on the landmark and follow his plan.
You are walking with truth and will hear shouts of Glory,
Join in the choir singing God's greatest love story.
   John 3:16

Generous Spirit

Ambrose
Delores
Dee
Doris
Galen
Grant
Gregory
Greg
Guy
Jason
Lola
Merle
Merlin
Miles
Missy
Misty
Mitzie
Phylis
Phyllis
Stewart
Steward

Generous One

Searching for answers, you check each day,
Wondering when life will change its way.
The ways of the world are wide and broad,
But your thoughts shall be of the Lord.
Straight and narrow are His actions and talk,
Yes with compassion you shall walk.
Did you know He hears your cry?
You are worthy to speak, don't be shy.
He only asks that you believe,
His only begotten Son we can receive.
He healed the broken hearted, Jesus is His name,
Tears He wept, this man without shame.
Compassion is what the Master gave to you,
You will spread it thru and thru.
To all who need a helping hand,
You will be there without demand.
Yes, you see the hurt among the people,
But your strength will come from His steeple.
Take your gift and use it well,
Compassion you have, this I can tell.
But greatest of all, keep looking to Him,
For He will lead you to blessings, filled to the brim.

Gentle With Compassion

Amos
Ampy
Avon
Carmella
Carmine
Coleen
Colleen
Dari
Gratton
Loma
Maranda
Mildred
Miranda
Myra
Ruth

Compassionate Spirit

Proud of family and friends and the life you live,
Gives you peace and comfort as you daily live.
Yes, gentleness is the path in life you walk,
Especially with those in contact you will talk.
Gentleness is giving attention without interrupting,
Completely polite, not disrupting.
A lesson to all you will show,
So gently move, as up the road you go.
You have been gentle to those who do good;
But wrath you show to those who have done no good.
Wrath shall be tempered by love,
Bringing wisdom, to keep back, within you to shove.
Every day is a new day for you, with hope,
Holding peace with comfort and not to grope.
God is pleased with a gentle spirit and heart,
Gentleness, it's only a very small part;
But for God to be pleased, is to mean we obeyed.
What great accomplishment Jesus surveyed.
So as you walk on His created sod,
Keep your eye upon our great Jehovah God.
His love for you will never die,
From day to day, on Him rely.

Industrious and Prosperous

Ashley
Ashton
Bartholomew
Bradley
Bradly
Dana
Felix
George
Georgia
Georgene
Georgine
Glenn
Gus
Henrietta
Henry
Milton
Milt
Sherman
Taylor
Teresa
Theresa
Todd
Tracy
Tyler
Vernon
Wallace
Wally
Webster
Wesley

Industrious and Prosperous

You are quite gentle, yet physically strong,
Interested in things of beauty will lead you along.
You strive for guidance and to study the unlearned,
Abundant life for all is why you are concerned.
For you know, there is a way to become a success,
That's why you want to share the hidden process.
You'll need to call on God, for strength from above,
Because success comes from Him, expressed by His love.
His encouraging words are needed each step of the way,
It's not easy to walk to a height, without play.
But you'll have time to relax and time to rest,
Just remember each day you must put forth your best.
You'll begin at the bottom and increase each day;
It will take hard work, enduring to get top pay.
And in the end when you have reached success,
Then you can pass to others for you have passed the test.
Don't forget to thank God, for His love he sent from above.
For it was Him who gave you wisdom on the wings of love.
Share the good news of Jesus, God's only begotten Son,
And tell of His kingdom in Heaven, where we will all be "one".

Gift of God

Dawson
Dora
Dorothea
Dorothy
Jan
Jana
Janell
Janet
Joan
Joane
Joanna
Joana
Matthew
Nathan
Nathanael
Nathaniel
Regina
Sylvester
Theodore
Woodrow
Woodwill

Gift of God

A gift of God is what your name means,
So you are here to please God, it seems.
Have you ever thought the plan for life,
And how you are to live without strife.
Free from jealousy, envy and scorn,
That's some of the reasons why you were born.
Treasures are in heaven, not earthly things that rust,
A lesson you learned, on the Father you can trust.
Yes, God does love you, blessings you can count,
And you will find them on His Holy mount.
Trying your best each day to keep things mild,
You are a peacemaker and called his child.
It is an honor to be called a gift of God, my friend,
For that means you are worthy for Him to send.
To tell the story of God's son to the people,
They are free to go hear His word at the steeple.
You have a quality not to get depressed,
Because on each subject, you dwell not to obsess.
Great are the battles you will fight,
They show the difference of wrong and right.
Remember each day to have no despair,
For your creator God, is with you everywhere.

God Is Judge

Blake
Daniel
Dan
Derek
Derrick
Rex
Russel
Russell
Winifred
Winnie

God Is Judge

A quiet nature, but you have many words to speak.
All bundled up inside of you waiting a time to seek.
A time to express yourself to someone who will listen,
Then comfort can go to your heart and your face will glisten.
Yes, you want justice and to see things done fair.
But sometimes the knocks of life will give you a scare.
For all things do not turn out fair and just,
Just rely that God is judge of everything, that's a must.
Did you know you have a pure heart within you,
That is why you see the goodness that others do.
You are worth a precious price to God above,
And all His angels are watching over you with love.
Isn't it good, that God is judge to hear and see over all,
Even in your darkest moments, he will always hear your call,
So stand up for justice, it entwines like a cord,
And shows forth the light of Jesus our Lord.
Justice is your quality, come forth with all your might,
One day you'll be glad to know you have done all in God's sight.
Yes, little master hold tight to the cord,
It shall entwine you with the love of the Lord.

Hell

1 Corinthians 15:55-57

Oh death where is thy sting? Oh grave where is thy victory?

The sting of death is sin and the strength of sin is the law.

But thanks be to God, which giveth us the victory through our Lord Jesus Christ.

Revelation 20:13

And death and hell were cast into the lake of fire. This the second death, and whosoever was not found in the book of life was cast into the lake of fire.

"The Lake of Fire"

"Eternal Torment Day and Night"
Revelation 20:10

God's Gracious Gift

Dohn
Edith
Evan
John
Johan
Johnann
Johanna
Jonathan
Jonette
Jon
Juan
Juanita
Marlow
Marlowe
Natasha
Omega
Oprah
Orpha
Otha
Otis
Reuben
Ruben
Rueben
Sean
Shane
Shawn

God's Gracious Gift

God has given you patience, his gracious gift,
And will use you to help others as they need a lift.
Patience is to endure delay without complaining,
And waiting for answers without restraining.
Tolerating commotion, knowing peace is sure to come,
It's time to share your patience, so each battle can be won.
You are part of God's plan, so give Him what is due,
Then you can find peace and contentment and not be blue.
We are only here in this world for a short life span,
And on to be with the Father, to a Holy land.
A place of beauty, health, truth, holiness and peace,
Your time of waiting will be over, and time on earth will cease.
Then comes heaven, when you shall see Jesus, God's only son,
That's where real treasures lay, and in his fullness we become.
But while her in this world, a peculiar one you are sealed,
And the Father's love is the only love, true and real.
So lift up your eyes toward heaven, the enemy you'll smite,
Just love God the Father with all of your might.
It's time to reap the Harvest and awake those that sleep,
For time is short and we must not leave any here to weep.
You have wisdom and discern the coming time-
He's coming back to gather His own and you'll see His love entwine.

God's Princess

Auderia
Audrey
Audey
Breck
Deana
Deanna
Gladys
Glecy
Sadie
Sally
Sarah
Sara
Sarena
Sharon
Shavone
Shavona
Zenobia

God's Princess

God calls you His little princess,
A daughter of the most high sovereign.
Your prince rules over principality,
And is an overseer in your locality.
Now there are good and evil kingdoms,
Make sure you are in lineage with the Prince of Peace.
For a princess stands by her Prince without cease.
So be careful little Princess,
For there is an evil kingdom, too;
And His rules will be unfair to you.
He rules the thoughts and it called, Prince of the air.
But there is one greater,
Who keeps us from the snare;
He paid the price, so you could be treated fair.
Jesus is His name, The Prince of Peace.
Frees you from the tempter,
Who ruins and destroys each and every plan
You have, because he is so coy.
But Jesus is greater, a man without sin;
He have His life so you could have complete dominion;
Oh, little princess, do you know you are loved?
By the one who is in power, from the King above.

Gracious

Ann
Anne
Annie
Anna
Annette
Anette
Antoinette
Antonia
Anita
Charissa
Clara
Dorcus
Hannah
Imogene
Jane
Janie
Jennifer
Jenifer
Kelly
Kelley
Lana
Lourdes
Maureen
Melinda
Nancy
Nanette

God's Grace

Gracious and Holy in the Father's eyes,
He looks on you, a handmaiden with no disguise.
Gracious is kindness and charm,
Giving your all to share with an upholding arm.
But sometimes you feel just like the stones,
Searching God's word to rise up your bones.
And so you read life's living word,
A gift to you, that you may serve.
It does free your spirit and uplift your heart,
For you have found out that this is your part.
Your strength is when on the Lord you wait,
Because you see the vision of the Holy gate.
He shall keep you, from within you to shove,
It's His promise of mercy, from the Father's love.
When you expose your heart to Him to sob,
His comforting no one will He allow to rob.
You are a pleasure to the Lord this day,
As He calls, you shall bow down to His way.
Laugh, cry, rejoice, be silent before Him,
You'll see His intimate to fill each whim.
More grace outpouring, He will bestow,
For you are His beloved, on His written scroll.

Inner Beauty

Belva
Bonita
Bonnie
Fara
Farley
Farrah
Inez
Ingrid
Jerusha
Linda
Roan
Roanna
Roanne
Sandra
Sondra

Inner Beauty

Beauty is the meaning of your name,
Judging without and within is your little game.
You strive for inner beauty and cast the hidden flaws away,
Yes, weeding faults daily, is the game you play.
You keep the righteousness and the things of God,
And hold on to His guidance as your Rod.
Real beauty is within the heart to show, Especially when the great winds begin to blow.
Wind can change one's beauty and charm,
But remember righteousness, nothing can harm.
Unshakeable is your beauty, for it is planted deep,
Don't carry that burden, go ahead and weep.
The Father will hear your cry and cuddle your heart,
Just give Him your cares, that's a good start.
He will give you beauty, as you look to Him,
And answer your call at the slightest whim.
You are His child and He watches you in this game you play,
Give Him your love and a smile from without and within today.

Joyous

Abigail
Blythe
Gwendolyn
Ida
Ilene
Joy
Joyce
Melody
Natalie
Noel
Tamela
Tammy

Joyous

It's easy to see what's on your mind,
You aim to please, for you are kind.
For in your eyes are a joy within,
Even when the going gets rough again.
You do not share what's on your mind,
For you think it's not important to whimp and whine.
But sometimes it's good to let off steam,
A sweet peace, better than you could dream.
Search your heart deep down inside,
It's the place our Father does reside.
Even in the secret places of your heart,
He dwells there quietly to be a part.
Rest in Him and leave an open door,
His love must freely move, for you to score.
You will come when on Him you can praise,
For all things He can do, your life He will raise.
Life will be easy to walk, but don't stray,
His love will guide you this very day.
Lean on Him or your time will be wasted,
You'll understand better after you've tasted.
A lesson is learned when you can do what is right,
For His grace is yours with His power and might.
Oh how He loves you, and unending band,
Keep your eye on Jesus, till you walk hand in hand.

Spirit of God

1 John 4:1-

Beloved, believe not every spirit, but try the spirits whether they are of God, because many false prophets are gone out into the world.

Hereby know ye the spirit of God; every spirit that confesseth that Jesus has come in the flesh, is of God.

And every spirit that confesseth not that Jesus has come in the flesh, is not of God, and his spirit is the Antichrist, whereof ye have heard that it should come; and even now already it is in the world.

Ye are of God little children and have overcometh them, because greater is He that is in you than he that is in the world.

They are of the world, therefore they speak of the world and the world heareth them. We are of God, he that knoweth God heareth us; he that is not of God heareth us not. Hereby reconcile to the spirit of truth.

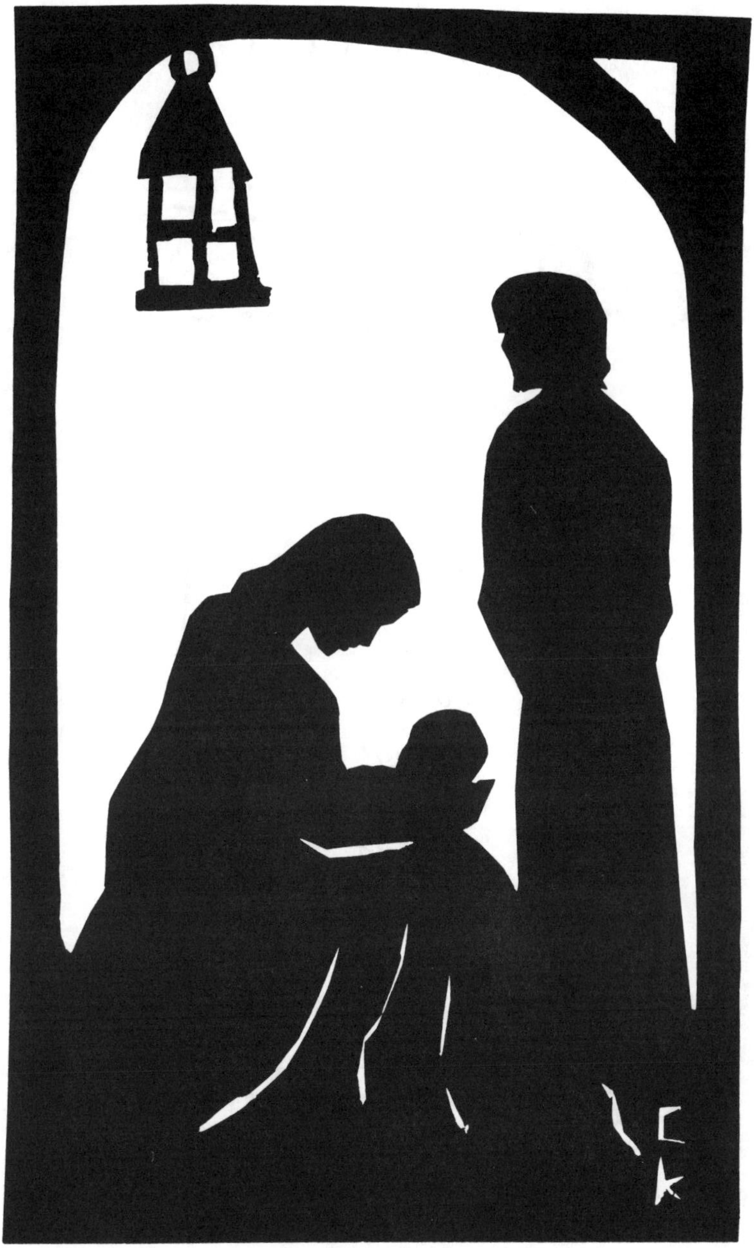

Lady of Victory

Bernice
Bernita
Brigette
Brittany
Bunnie
Carmillia
Colette
Collette
Deneal
Elouise
Lois
Louise
Marissa
Nel
Stasha

Lady of Victory

It's a wonder to me why you always win,
Then one day I realized, your name means Victory, the one to win.
You helmet, shield and sword is on before each battle you begin.
The helmet of saving grace, your shield of faith, able to quench the fiery darts,
Having on the breastplate of righteousness, carrying your sword of truth to win.
No wonder you have the battle won before you begin.
Your name is Victory and your feet walk in peace;
Battle scars heal, while Victory shall increase.
Settle down now, don't let Victory overthrow,
The humbleness you need most to show.
Humbleness is a trait of strength, which will rule the world one day.
Never forget these words to you I say.
Remember humbleness!
Victory is to conquer, humbleness is kind.
Humbleness, my precious friend, cannot be left behind.

Commandments

Matthew 22:36-40

Master, which is the greatest commandment? Jesus said unto him, Thou shall love the Lord thy God with all your heart, all your soul and all of your mind.

This is the first and the great commandment and the second is like unto it, love thy neighbor as thy self. On these two commandments; hang all the law and the prophets.

Matthew 5:17-18

Think not that I have come to destroy the law or the prophets. I am come to fulfill my word.

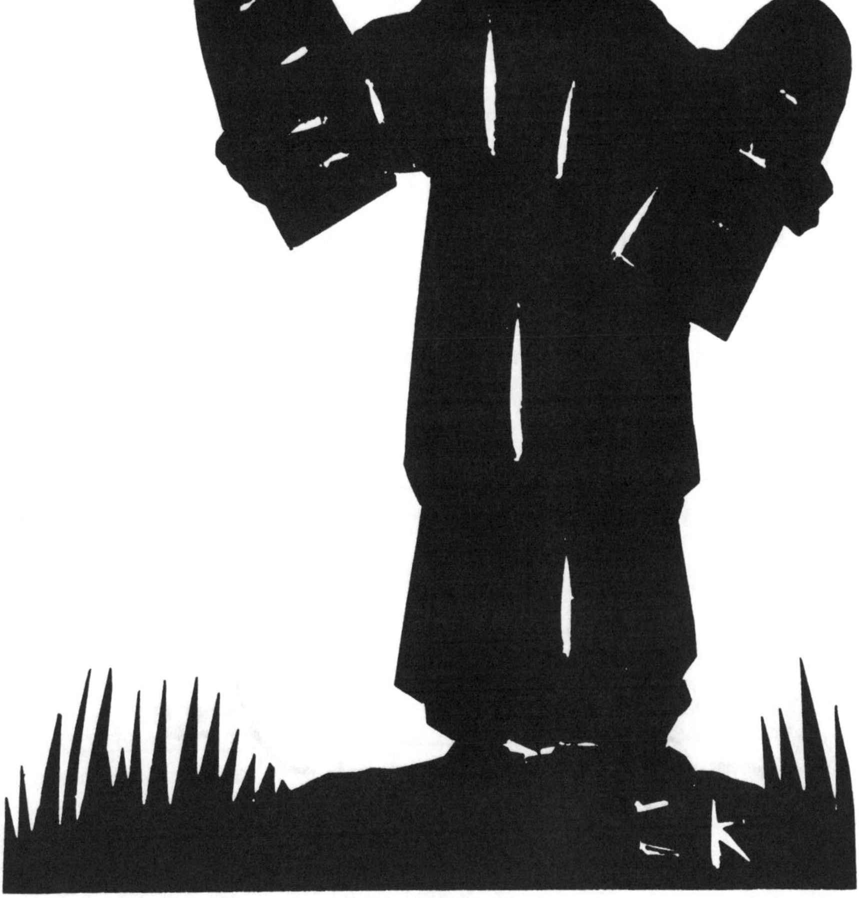

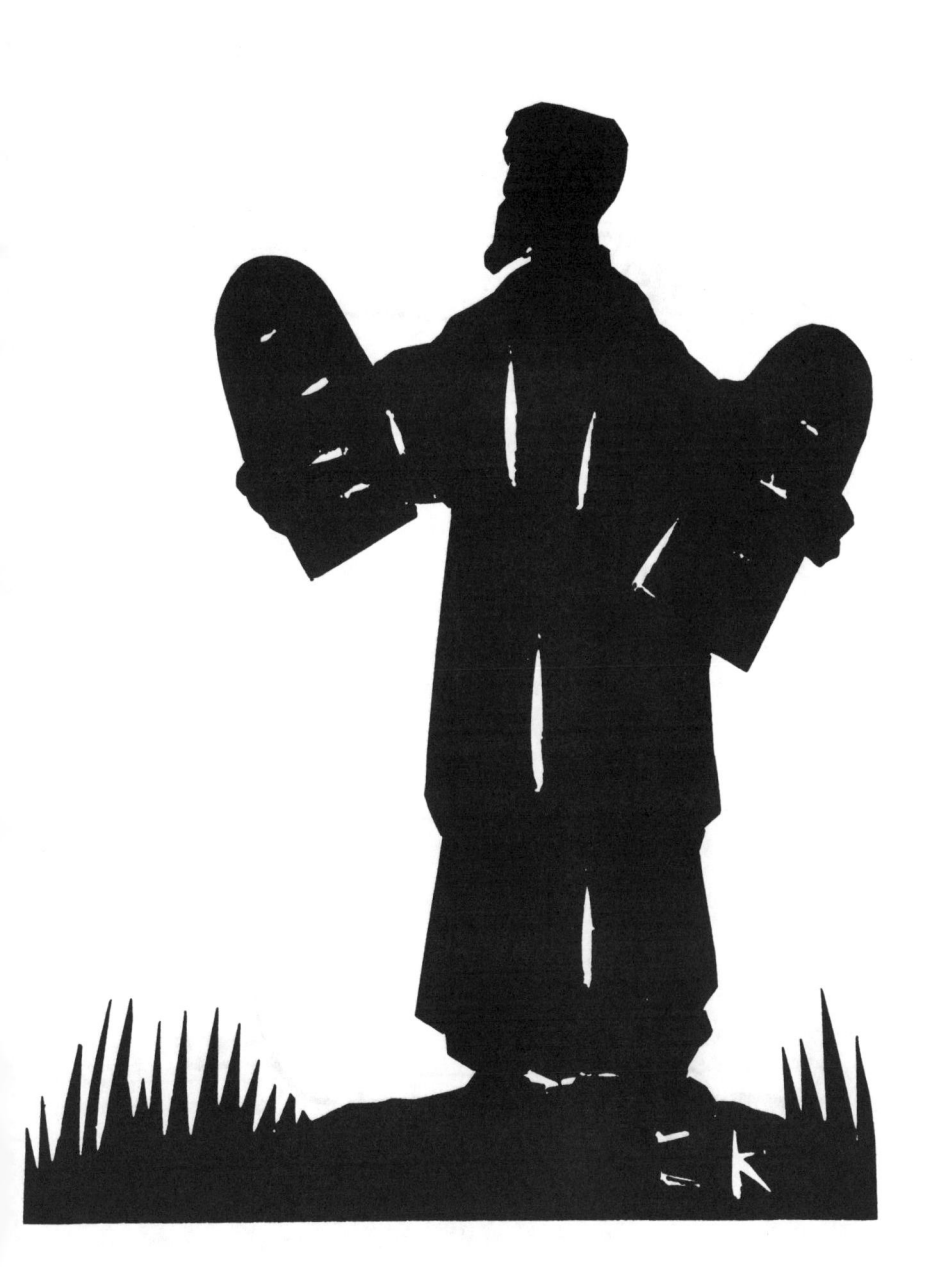

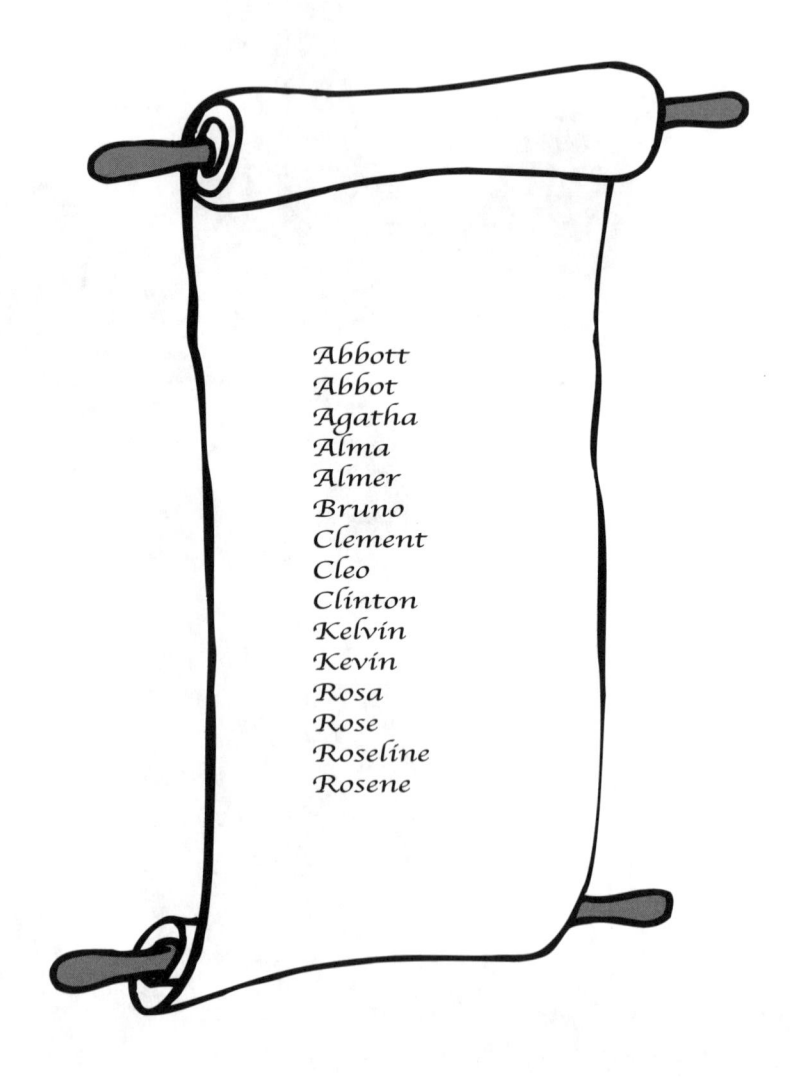

Loving and Kind

Abbott
Abbot
Agatha
Alma
Almer
Bruno
Clement
Cleo
Clinton
Kelvin
Kevin
Rosa
Rose
Roseline
Rosene

Loving and Kind

As the jewels do sparkle and shine,
Does your love for others reach out sublime.
Caring sometimes to a point of dismay,
Remember to pray, your answer is on the way.
Rest in Him to handle your prayer,
And make it real, they're in His care.
Your heart will lift when you look above,
Jesus will send His peace, quiet like the dove.
You know His love, great things you have learned;
A cry to the Father a lesson discerned.
Your love is complete to see the story end,
His rewards in heaven He will send.
Genuine as rubies and diamonds with beautiful sparkle to compare,
That's the way your love for others is portrayed, radiant and sincere.
I pray to the Father that you will be filled,
With all the love returned to you.
As you freely give, receive unto you.
It's His will to love one another each day,
To do His purpose and His plan without delay.
So I thank our Father for you,
And the love you will share so true.

Loyal

Boris
Brett
Duncan
Dustin
Ellery
Elmer
Eugene
Gary
Gene
Gerard
Gerold
Giles
Harvey
Herman
Horace
Marlin
Marshall
Randal
Randall
Randolph
Rudolph
Scott

Loyal One

Loyal to all, that you should touch,
It's important that you care so much.
For everyone really needs to endure,
And to be strong, so no one can lure.
If you set your mind to get something done,
You can bet your life, because Victory is won.
Just strive for the goal, you will not fail,
And no one can say they heard you wail.
Getting your way is not easily done,
Keep lifting your voice, it will come.
Make sure your way is fair and just,
Or there will be turmoil, that's a must.
For God above judges each and every heart,
And in this world we all have a part.
Give what you have, it's called, loyal,
And you shall be treated as tho Royal.
You know the story of Jesus, God's son,
And how He wants us all to be one.
For this He died and gave His life,
That in this world, we should have no strife.
Carry on, you are a child of the King,
And in the heavens, one day you'll sing.

Mighty and Powerful

Adolph
Adolf
Alaph
Aloph
Barney
Brant
Brent
Burton
Burt
Dale
Erick
Erik
Gertrude
Gordon
Marcelle
Mark
Martin
Norman
Rain
Raine
Reynold
Rhea
Ronald
Troy
Trudi
Trudy
Yvonne

Mighty and Powerful

To reign is your desire with power,
Be careful though of the evil mighty tower.
It persuades and entices without a fight,
Until even the wrongs seem right.
You are a child of God, a price was paid for you,
Keep your eye on the Savior, He will guide you through.
Walk in the steps He has already prepared,
And the life together, He has shared.
A special quality, you have a giving heart,
A gift to you, but it's only a part.
With it comes kindness and mercy, too;
A touch from your heart will make one coo.
You see you learned the secret word,
The one received by all unless unheard.
"Love", the word that melts the heart,
Respect this word when said it's a powerful start.
To reign in love, is to hurt no one,
Our greatest example is God's only Son.
So rise up now and reign in love,
And God will send His blessing from above.

Nobel and Honorable

Albert
Alberta
Candace
Candice
Earl
Eli
Gilbert
Heidi
Hubert
Jay
Noble
Nora
Norah
Noreen
Norienne
Norma
Patricia
Tricia
Patrick
Raynor
Samuel
Tania
Tonya
Teva
Weeks
Wilber
Wilbur

Full of Honor

Honor is integrity, earning the greatest respect,
It seems to be surrounding you, can you detect?
It's you who have the reputation to do good,
And you who will gain honor, that's understood.
Honor is to have high regards for action displayed,
Someone who shows his personality to all arrayed.
Holding high the qualities, to put others first,
Standing on a firm righteousness, you do thirst.
These characteristics come from God above,
He will guide you and teach you of His love.
Remember not to brag, in honor there is no space;
Respect is earned quietly in it proper place.
You won't have to lift yourself up high,
You will be honored for your action draweth nigh.
Keep your temper cool, and rest secure,
For there are many who will try to lure.
Beware and discern the difference of peace,
So you can go on to be honored without cease.
Now it is time for you to become brave and bold,
And on these qualities you shall behold.
It's right and just for you to be seen,
As a person of honor, this is no dream.
So be brave and bold and righteous inside,
For the Father, God, in your heart does reside.

Obedient

Dimeon
Ezra
Paige
Ramona
Simeon
Simon
Dimeon
Tina
Tinica
Tineka
Trevor
Zepy

Obedient Spirit

Guess you know it's time to relax,
To sit down and begin to gather facts.
Organized with life is neatly put,
But can you rest today each foot.
Always your daily chores, you do your best.
Receive your rewards, you pass the test.
Obedience has been a strong character you hold,
But I pray you keep within God's fold.
Sometimes we lean to our own understanding,
But His lasting word, He remains standing.
A friend you've been to me, I didn't expect.
I cherish your help to me, plus your respect.
It's needed, you know, to have a friend like you,
One to talk with and share a happiness, too.
For you see, it's only a short life we live;
Nothing can we keep, only our life to give.
Learning, caring, and believing here,
That we might see heaven's stair.
Consequences of life all come together now,
Keep giving your heart and humbly bow.

Obedience

Acts 5:29
And then Peter said we ought to obey God rather than men.

"Noah Obeyed God Rather Than Men"

Genesis 6:22
"And Noah did according unto all that the Lord commanded him."

Proverbs 3:25-26

Be not afraid of sudden fear, neither of the desolation of the wicked when it cometh.

For the Lord shall be thy confidence and shall keep thy foot from being taken.

Matthew 14:27
Be of good cheer; it is I; be not afraid.

Mark 5:36
Be not afraid only believe.

Peaceful Spirit

Freda
Irene
Leah
Lee
Leigh
Leslie
Lesley
LeAnne
Olive
Olivia
Shirley
Sheryl

Peaceful Spirit

You are a woman of compassion and endurance to bring peace.
A sensitive touch for others is a gift that will not cease.
Because you are a peacemaker, you are called a child of God.
That's not to say that sometimes you would rather carry a rod.
Your long spans of time in thought are moments that cannot be bought.
For others could learn from you to take time and do as you do.
It's a special quality you've had that will bring you good instead of bad.
Always know that as you gaze, seek wisdom in all your ways.
Then they will know, you are weighing things out;
In the eyes of God, that's what it's all about.
Starting from birth, till death you'll see.
It's God's pleasure for you to be,
The woman of compassion and endurance, of peace for all to see.

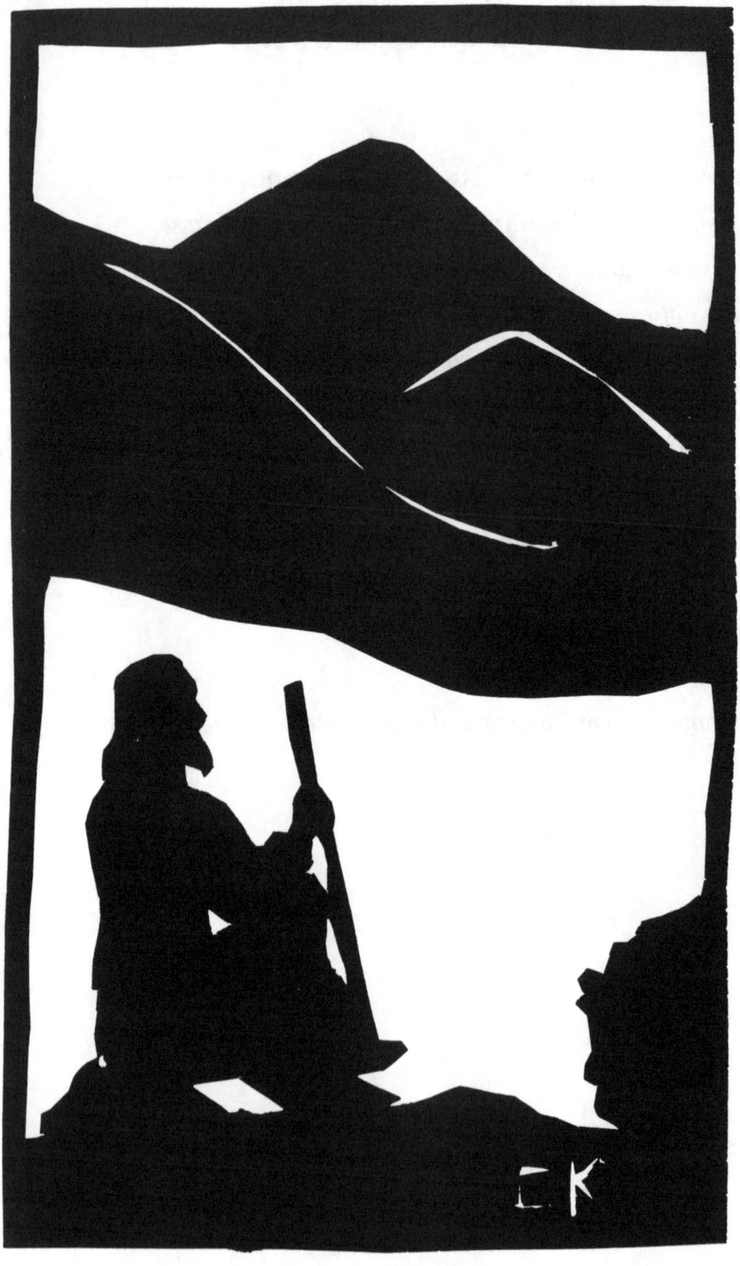
EK

Quietness

Ecclesiastes 4:6
Better is a handful with quietness, than both the hands full with travail and vexation of spirit.

1 Peter 3:4
But let it be the hidden man of the heart, in that which is not corruptible, even the ornament of a meek and quiet spirit, which is in the sight of God, a great price.

Pearl

Agnes
Amber
Darren
Darrin
Genevieve
Ginger
Gretchen
Laverne
Margaret
Margarete
Margarita
Margo
Margaritte
Margot
Marjorie
Marge
Marlisa
Marilyn

A Pearl

Quiet in Spirit, you are known,
But shouts of Glory come when full grown.
A helper to all, when given a chance,
You are not worried, to who might glance.
A pearl in the eyes of the Father today.
Costly, pure and one of a kind I say.
Did you ever think He did not notice you?
The one who is called, faithful and true.
Unique to God, but to others odd,
Because you do no purpose to carry a rod.
A rod is by force without a choice,
But you do it your way by lifting your voice.
It takes longer your way, for discipline;
But lasting forever, a decision to win.
It's plain to see, your Bible gathers no dust,
For it's on His word, you put your trust.
Your life is seen by angels unaware,
So you see the facts are shown completely bare.
And what you do each day is a test,
Till when you shout "Glory," you'll know
Then, you entered His rest.

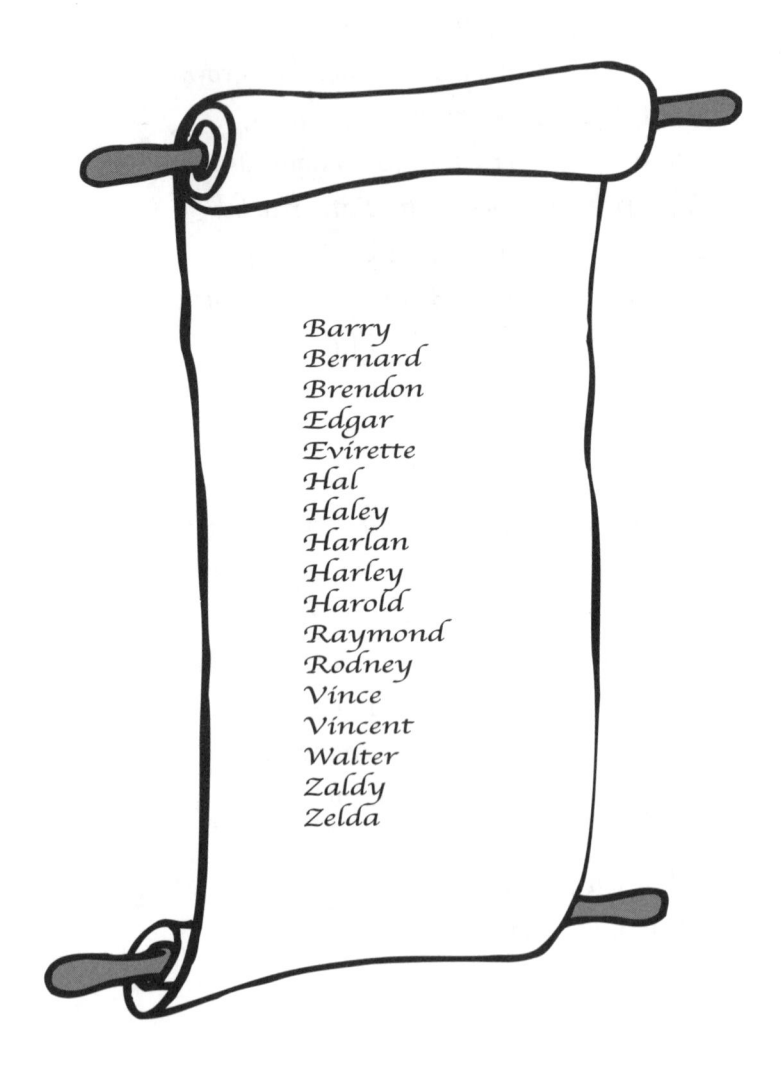

Powerful Spirit

Barry
Bernard
Brendon
Edgar
Evirette
Hal
Haley
Harlan
Harley
Harold
Raymond
Rodney
Vince
Vincent
Walter
Zaldy
Zelda

Powerful Spirit

Even tho quiet natured with your fellow man,
Your influence is powerful, when you take a stand.
For everything is thought over, before you speak,
And on the Father's love you try to seek.
A man devoted to the family ties,
Will keep you busy, for you hear their cries.
Comfort you will be, bringing peace,
And praying that all evil will cease.
Did you know you touch the heart of God,
On you He does not have to use a rod.
For you are submissive to His call,
Just remember, He will not let you fall.
Jesus is the only begotten Son of God,
Our example, when we walk this sod.
So stay within the Father's reach,
That He may show you what to teach.
Your influence is powerful, when you take a stand,
And needed much, that you should lend a hand.
Our Lord is like a burning consuming fire,
Purging you thoroughly till you call Him "the Messiah".
What great love is this above?
It's God our Father, Jesus and the heavenly dove.

Precious

Alta
Cheri
Cherise
Delia
Delilah
Delton
Jewel
Kerry
Ketukah
Larita
Marlea
Mel
Melba
Nona
Peggy
Percy
Rita
Sheri
Sherry

Precious One

A precious pearl, born of God
As is your life, to walk His sod.
Rare and pure till you get old
Beauty from your heart, is to behold.
Life is easy when you look up
The steps you take are but his cup.
A strength within comes forth to you
Just when it's impossible to see things through.
All the tears you have cried are worth it all
For you have seen beyond the wall.
As in His path, is life above
And from His son, the gift of love.
When you served God and heard His call
You knew He would not let you fall.
And now I think my god above
That He shares with us the wings of love.

Priceless and Strong

Anthony
Antony
Antonio
Tony
Arron
Augustus
Benjamin
Bud
Charles
Chuck
Charlie
Clarence
Kendall
Kent
Meagan
Rhea
Tony

Priceless and Strong

Did you know you are called a priceless one,
And any Father would be proud to call you son.
You work so hard and it's appreciated much,
Do you realize how many lives you touch?
You work sometimes until you call out a sigh,
But I know someone who can lift you high.
It's God the Father who knows each care,
And to Him you can go with a fervent prayer.
For He loves you and He loves me, too,
And doesn't want any of us to feel blue.
You are extra strong, this I know,
But we all do need much more to grow.
Our hearts do break and need to mend,
That's why the Savior He did send.
His help is there, when on Him you call,
With love He can break down any wall.
Yes, Jesus already received the scorn,
So in us a new life would be born.
He paid the price, that His Son would become,
Oh priceless one, hear the Father call you son.

Innerman

Ephesians 3:16-19

That he would grant you according to the riches in Glory, to be strengthened with might by his spirit in the innerman. That Christ may dwell in your hearts by faith, that ye may comprehend with all saints, what is the breadth the length the depth and the height; and to know the love of Christ which passeth all knowledge, that ye might be filled with the fullness of God. Now to him that is able to do exceedingly abundantly above all that we ask or think, accordingly to the power that works in us.

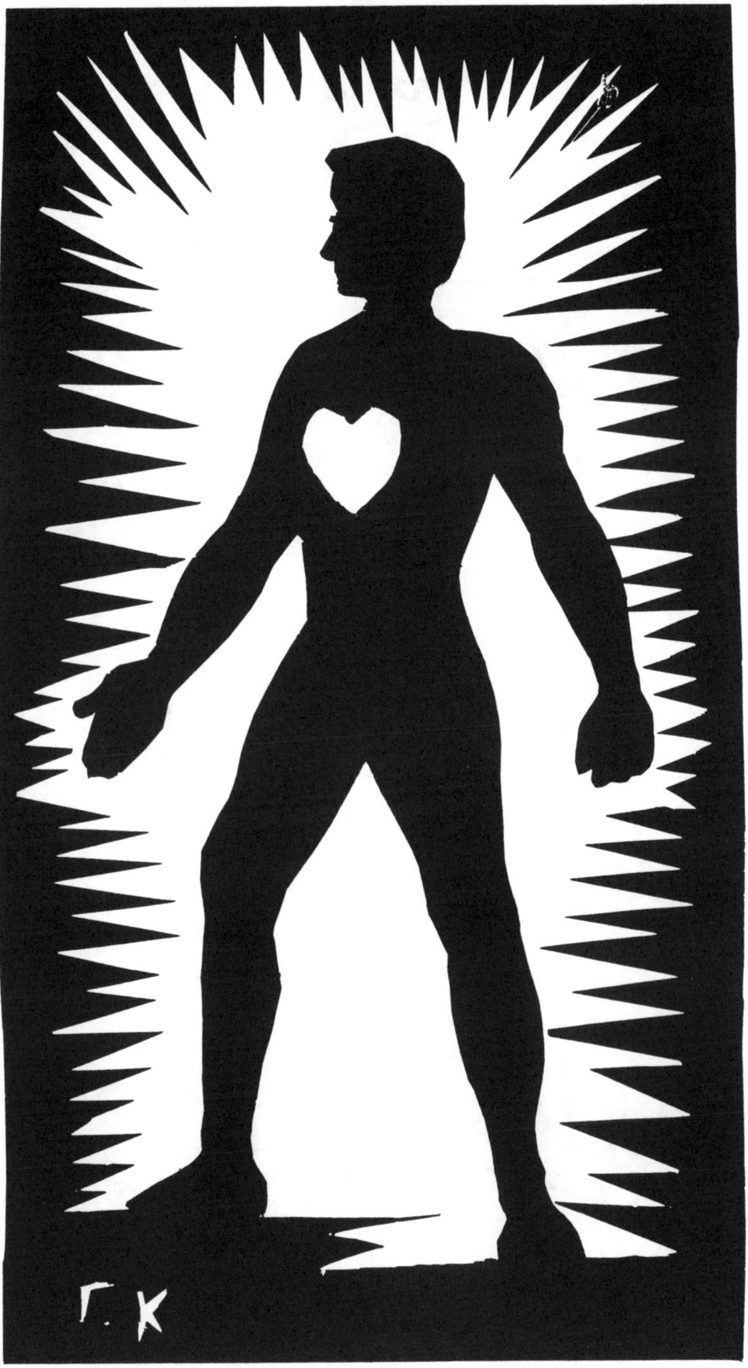
Г. К

Protector

Abraham
Abram
Alexander
Alex
Chad
Chester
Edmond
Edmund
Edna
Edward
Edwin
Hester
Marlin
Shelly
Shelley
Ted
Tedmund
Warner
Warren
William
Willie Mae
Bill
Wilma

Prosperous Protector

A great protector is your way of charm,
To search for ways and keep from harm.
You feel you must hold up a shield,
A cover for those included in your field.
Protector is security who declares the alarm,
And renders a place with a faithful arm.
Sometimes you get weary and want to give up,
And wish to be pampered like a small pup.
Why so you have such a hard time to relay,
You get so involved to a point of dismay.
But it's all right, you can recoup,
Just enjoy the happenings of your group.
Be silent and point to heaven with your eyes,
There is much to see in the quiet if the skies.
It will brighten your day and bring new hope,
There will be no reason for you to grope.
A beauty to stir the heart, to sweet peace,
And to those around calamity will cease.
Take time to relax, a prayer you can say,
You'll find out you are loved in the highest way.
Loved by the Father, who created us all,
Will give you comfort and break down the wall.
To reach you, in the oneness of Him,
Then pour out His blessings filled to the brim.

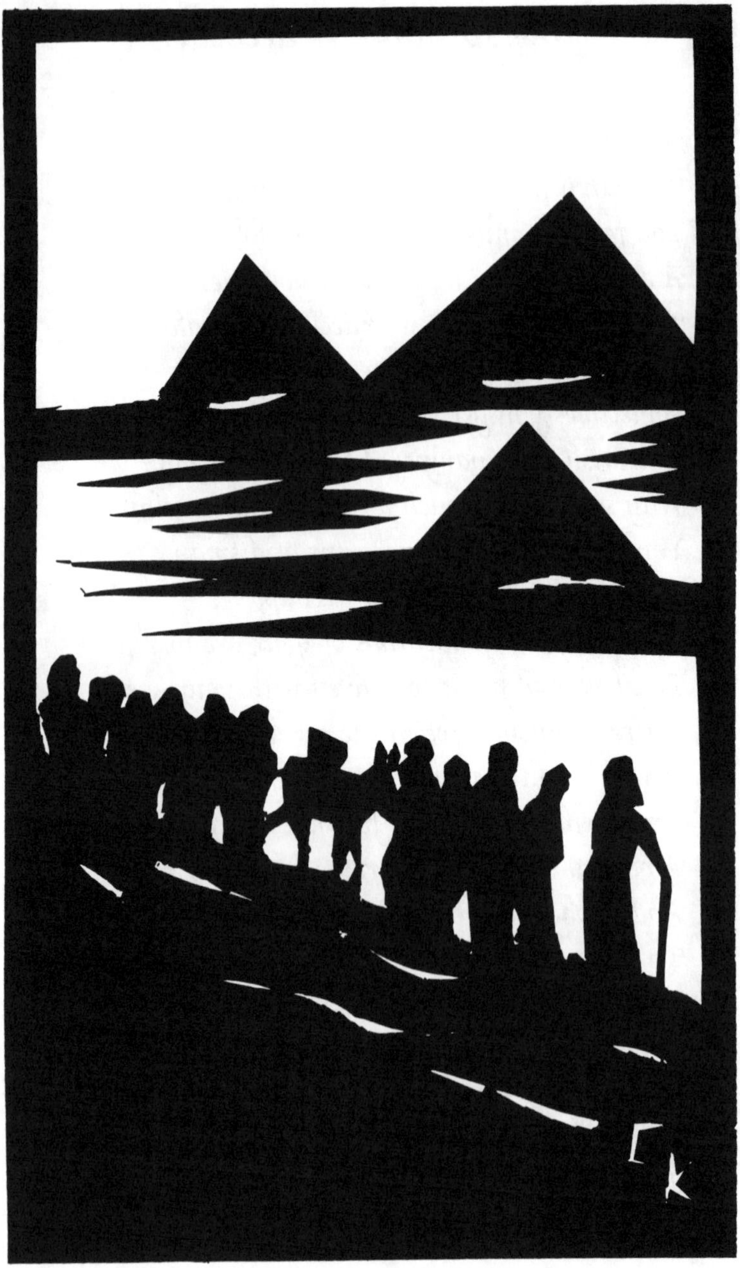

Led From Bondage

Exodus 2:23-24

And it came to pass in the process of time, that the King of Egypt died and the children of Israel sighed by reason of bondage and their cry came up to God by reason of bondage.

And God heard their groaning and God remembered his Covenant with Abraham with Isaac and with Jacob.

And God looked on the children of Israel and had respect unto them.

1 Peter 2-9-10

But you are a chosen generation, a royal priesthood a Holy nation, a peculiar people that ye should show the praises of Him who has called you out of darkness into His marvellous light.

Purity In Thought

Blanche
Catherine
Katherine
Cathy
Kathy
Cathleen
Kathleen
Catrina
Katrina
Courtney
Danette
Danielle
Holly
Karen
Karin
Katherlyn
Kathryn
Katie
Katy
Kay
Lavelle
Lavina
Martha
Melissa
Pamela
Pearl
Pearle
Ruby
Virginia

Pure

A quiet nature, but you have many words to speak.
All bundled up inside of you waiting a time to seek.
A time to express yourself to someone who will listen
Then comfort can go to your heart and your face will glisten.
Yes, you want justice and to see things done fair.
But sometimes the knocks of life will give you a scare.
For all things will not turn out fair and just,
Just rely that God is judge of everything, that's a must.
Did you know you have a pure heart within you,
That's why you see the goodness that others do.
You are worth a precious price to God above,
And all his angels are watching over you with love.
Isn't it good, that God is judge to hear and see over all,
Even in your darkest moments, he will always hear your call.
So stand up for justice, it entwines like a cord,
And shows forth the light of Jesus our Lord.
Justice is your quality, come forth with all your might,
One day you'll be glad to know you have done all in God's sight.
Yes, little daughter hold tight to the cord,
It shall entwine you with the love of the Lord.

Quiet Spirit and Declarer of God

Angus
Hazel
Iva
Ivan
Iverna
Joel
Naomi
Penny
Shannon
Zachariah
Zechariah
Zachary

Quiet Spirit   Declarer of God

Day by day you live your life to do your very best,
Being faithful to declare God's word is when you enter rest.
Yes, you know truth and what the Bible reveals,
God's word is faithful and nothing does he conceal.
You don't have to be perfect, only honest and true,
Then a peace within will come and satisfaction, too.
You are a child of God and in His kingdom you'll stay;
God is worthy of all your praise, to Him in all array.
Your quiet and gentle spirit is precious in His sight,
For God himself moves by His spirit not by might.
Declare glory unto God, for His mercy and grace forever endures,
Yet you must be careful against temptation where evil lures.
Satan is a deceiver, a destroyer of God's Holy word,
So get your armor on and live today the Holy word you've learned.
Love is the greatest weapon entwined with truth spoken out,
It releases and sets the captive free, that's what truth is all about.
You cannot hide your heart and what it holds inside,
For there is one greater who dwells within to reside.
Did you think you were forgotten and obsolete?
Not by any means, God the father only wants to make you complete.

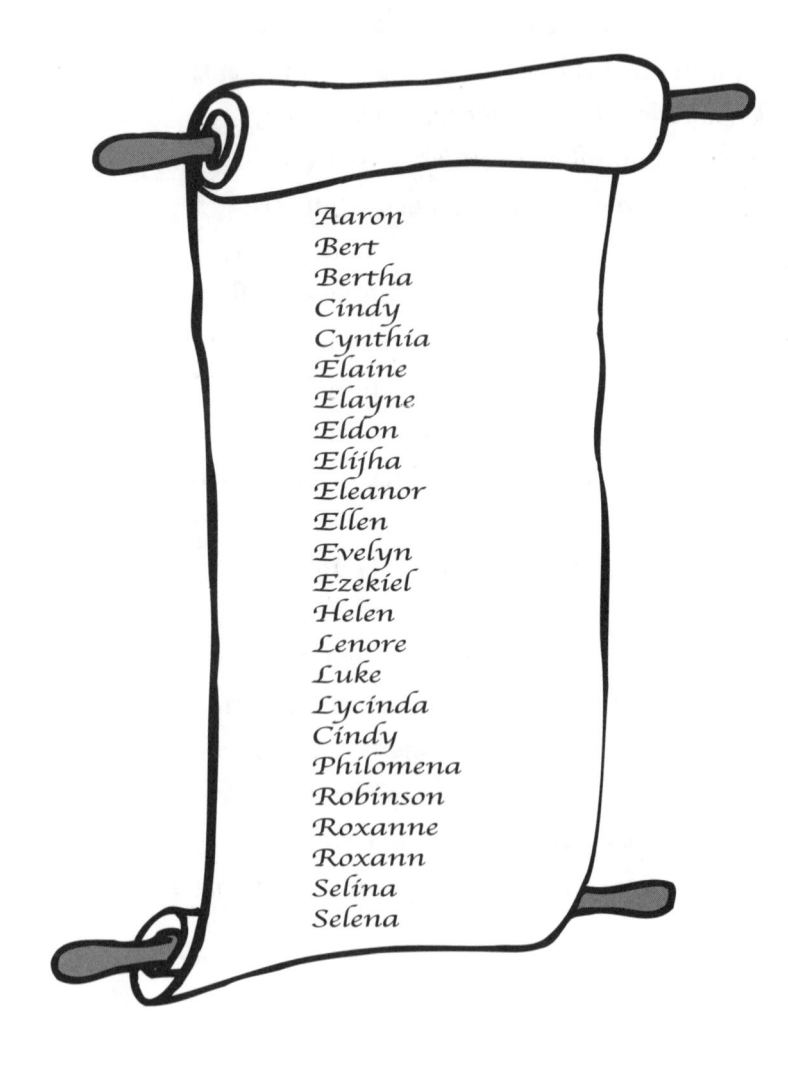

Reflector of Light

Aaron
Bert
Bertha
Cindy
Cynthia
Elaine
Elayne
Eldon
Elijha
Eleanor
Ellen
Evelyn
Ezekiel
Helen
Lenore
Luke
Lycinda
Cindy
Philomena
Robinson
Roxanne
Roxann
Selina
Selena

Reflector of Light

Reflector of light is the meaning of your name,
Match up the personality, till it becomes the same.
Light shines in the darkness, when no one can see,
It's important for you to be all that you can be.
Light radiates a path to guide the steps to what's ahead,
Just know that you reflect the light and remember what I said.
Righteousness is your intention and you strive to fulfill,
Sometimes it gets tough on you for temptations break your will.
Be strong and know God will give you strength and mend
Each problem and each care you have, His help He's sure to send.
You have a love for people, but let it grow inside.
Till you can see and feel in your heart God does reside.
Yes, you are a reflector of light, it will bounce to others,
Just like little children reflect lessons from their mothers.
People learn from the reflection, sometimes good, sometimes bad,
So reflect your light of good intentions, then you won't be sad.
You have a way of cheering those, especially who have a need.
These are the actions showing light, and a very good deed.
You are a child of God, He gave His son, because of you;
Jesus is His name, your greatest example, to subdue.
Reflector of light, take your stand and walk hand in hand,
You have your example, there is no greater man.

Love

Luke 7:44-47

See this woman? I entered this house, thou gavest me no water for my feet, but she has washed my feet with tears and wiped them with the hairs of head.

Thou gavest me no kiss: but this woman since the time I came in hath not ceased to kiss my feet.

My head with oil, you did not anoint, but this woman has anointed my feet with ointment.

Wherefore I say unto thee, her sins which are many are forgiven; for she loveth much: but to whom little is forgiven, the same loveth little.

Love

1 Corinthians 13:3-8

And tho I bestow all my goods to the poor and tho I give my body to be burned and have no love, it profit nothing.

Love suffered long, Love is kind, Love does not envy, Love is not forceful, Love is not braggard, Love does not behave rudely, Love is not selfish, Love is slow to anger, Love thinketh no evil;

Love rejoiceth not in evil but rejoiceth in the truth. Love bears all things, Love hopes all things, Love endures all things, Love never fails.

Refreshing Cheerful Life

Abel
Al
Allen
Alan
Alton
Duane
Gillian
Ira
Isaac
Jasmine
Lacey
Lacie
Lark
Lincoln
Lindsay
Lyndon
Muray
Owen
Zoe

Refreshing Cheerful Life

Much like trees, you flourish and stand in beauty,
As the tree root is planted to fill its duty.
So it is with you, you grow, you mature,
To the fullness you were created to be.
Your cheerfulness spreads to those around,
While your joyful giggle pleases beyond its sound.
Patience tells me you are willing to wait for the very best,
Even to suffer, you pass the test.
God calls you His child and each tear He will understand,
Who can separate His love, it's like a wedding band.
Same as the "lily of the valley" blowing in the wind,
You are strong to stand tall, against the world's sin.
It's good to know someone like you,
The way you share and care for others, too.
Your beauty is rare and seen in the eyes of love.
From our Father up above.

Secure and Free

Alexis
Alexandria
Bruce
Darby
Frances
Francis
Frank
Franklin
Joshua
Keith
Silvia
Sylvia
Sybil
Zelma

Secure One

Did you know your name means secure one,
So you can rest assured freedom will come.
Free from danger, for you are highly protected,
Aren't you glad you were uniquely selected?
A price was paid so you could be free,
God gave His son Jesus, for you and me.
It's good to know you are free from harm,
And there is no reason for you to pull the alarm.
Just stay alert and believe in Jesus, God's son,
He gave His word to teach us, His own are "one".
One in Spirit; and one in his kingdom of love,
It was God our Father who sent Jesus from above.
To lead the way ahead and carry our load,
A straight and narrow way is the Lord's road.
So stay close to His teaching and let Him direct,
For it's Him who will carry you, and always protect.
Guess you know, when He comes back to get His own,
You'll be ready, for you have planted seeds to be sown.
His children are light, to the dark world around,
Shine bright each day, it's almost time for the trumpet sound.

Seeking One

Deborah
Debra
Delmar
Delma
Douglas
Dwight
Tamara
Tamera
Tandi
Tandy
Thomas
Tom
Tommy
Whitney

Seeker of Light

Can it be real, you seek truth from the Father's eyes,
Thru the dark clouds and silver linings so very high.
You are a truth seeker and you judge by God's word,
Sometimes it hurts, when truth needs to be heard.
But stronger you'll get, as you recieve from the heart,
A greater span of time for you to get your part.
You dwell in truth and soak in its savor;
Salt of the earth you are called to add flavor.
Taste and see if truth does not satisfy,
With a peace and contentment no one can deny.
Seeker of truth is a pleasure so rare,
To whom does it matter, as long as you care.
For the Father knows your heart my friend,
And on the wings of love, Jesus He'll send.
To help, to strengthen and your life He will mend.
Take courage and know that he is your friend.
Remember, be strong, for you are not alone,
To be tossed and turned as tho wind blown.
You are a child of the King this day,
Seeker of truth, you shall find your way.
A path so narrow, take one step at a time,
It will lead you to the Father, His love is not blind.
Who can say what the heart whispers within,
Only our Master who created you, gave you victory over sin.

Song of Joy

Carmen
Carol
Carolina
Claire
Clair
Eileen
Ella
Ellie
Eunice
Karoline
Lillian
Lilly
Lucile
Lucy
Muriel

Song of Joy

Strength like yours is hard to find
Leaving worldly riches far behind.
I see you twice, first like a lion roaring his commands,
Then as a lamb without any last demands.
Pure in heart right from the start,
You didn't know you had a part.
But soon found out your life was planned
By the Spirit of the Father, scanned.
Eternal light, you pass to others with the worlds of truth and grace;
Knowing in his presence abides the bright amazing grace.
Yes, you hear and see the sorrows of the people you hold dear,
Cling fast to the Savior, the one without fear,
Giving all He had so you could bear.
You sing a new song with the angels and the saints,
Spreading restoration to the world, a joy so quaint.
A light in the night is your song on time,
Bringing this echo from the Father, "She's mine."

Strength of Character

Donika
Donna
Ethel
Irvin
Griffin
Marsha
Rhoda
Rhonda
Robin
Sharlene

Strength of Character

There will be many doors for you and open gates
Because of your quality and durability as your traits.
Durability is long lasting, power to resist on attack.
So take notice of your quality, its your greatest contact.
Self respect is important in our daily walk in life,
Walk with honor, it will lead you from worry and strife.
There are a multitude of words, you've already been told
If you keep your eyes and ears open, then no one can scold.
Seek the Savior who loves you; while He is near,
He will guide you and lead you and be perfectly clear.
His words are strength to the character you hold.
It's about time for you to stand up and be bold.
Bold for the good and righteous opinion,
So that you can rule with peace in your dominion.
Since you are God's child, He will keep you in His care,
And direct you from falling within a snare.
So keep your eyes and ears open, ready to obey,
To listen for the words, that Jesus might say.
Yes, a short life we live, only to leave the memory behind
So share what you have and remember to be kind.

Strong and Manly

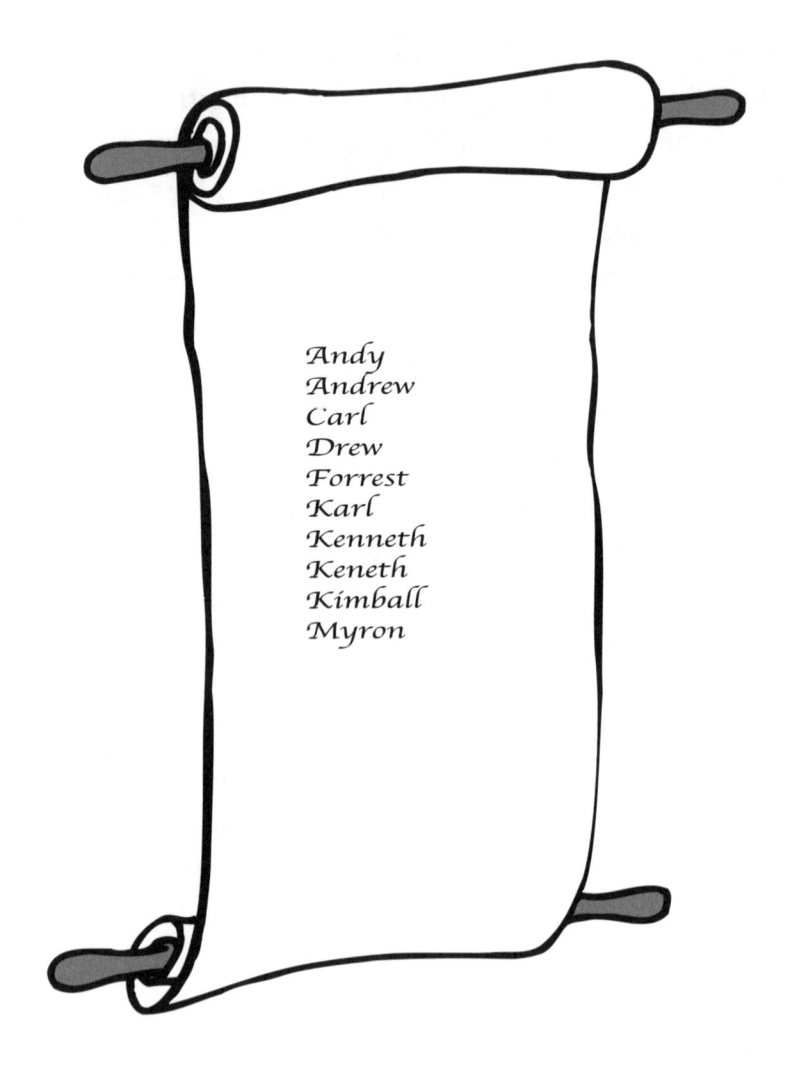

Andy
Andrew
Carl
Drew
Forrest
Karl
Kenneth
Keneth
Kimball
Myron

Strong Manly

Enduring daily, that's what makes you strong,
Deciding which way is right and which way is wrong.
A man of honor, calling our shouts of joy,
For you have seen reality and know life is not a toy.
But a place of learning and a time for us to see,
The love of God, the Father and His son Jesus, was He.
A perfect portrait of you is when you pray.
And His perfect will is to answer without delay.
So begin to thank Him, knowing He cares,
Believing it's done, will keep you from snares.
It's easy to speak and hear but a doer are you,
A doer is action, where your words become true,
Guess you know people are counting on you.
They look at your life to see what blessings come true.
It's wonderful how Jesus will not point the blame,
But can put your whole life in one picture frame.
Yes, a perfect portrait of you is when you pray,
And His perfect will is to answer without delay.
You see Jesus gave us His name to use,
And for those prayers the Father will choose.
Yes a servant, for the Lord today,
And on His written word you do obey.
Blessings will come your way as you believe,
Your part is to love the Father and receive.

Strong Womanly

Andrea
Andria
Benita
Bennita
Bernadette
Carrie
Carla
Carletta
Charlene
Cheryl
Hilda
Kimball
Kimberly
Kari
Karrie
Karla
Tabatha

Strong Womanly

Enduring daily, that's what makes you strong,
Deciding which way is right and which way is wrong.
A woman of honor, calling out shouts of joy,
For you have seen reality and know life is not a toy.
But a place of learning and a time for us to see,
The love of God, the Father, and His son Jesus, was He.
A perfect portrait of you is when you pray,
And His perfect will is to answer without delay.
So begin to thank Him, knowing He cares,
Believing it's done, will keep you from snares.
It's easy to speak and hear but a doer are you,
A doer is action, where your words become true,
Guess you know people are counting on you.
They look at your life to see what blessings come true.
It's wonderful how Jesus will not point the blame,
But can put your whole life in one picture frame.
Yes, a perfect portrait of you is when you pray,
And His perfect will is to answer without delay.
You see Jesus give us His name to use,
And for those prayers the Father will choose.
Yes, a handmaiden, for the Lord today,
And on His written word you do obey.
Blessings will come your way as you believe,
Your part is to love the Father and receive.

Transformed Good Steward

Bridgette
Cacey
Casey
Earlene
Ferdnard
Jill
Julie
Jule
Julia
Jullian
Julian
Julianna
Juliet
Julius
Mac
Madeline
Newman
Rocky
Spencer
Stacy
Stacey

Transformed Heart

You are considered strong and a faithful steward, too
One who takes care of matters and what belongs to you.
Have you looked at you today, do you see what I can see?
Take a look and see if you can agree with me.
Your kindness warmed a heart, when you displayed,
And your laughter tickled me, can this be true, you say?
So independent to do thins your way without sway,
Lean not to just your understanding, it might not be the way.
But lean to righteousness, a lesson you will discern,
Each answer has been tried, only righteousness is the concern.
Yes, I looked at you today and see the time we shared,
I appreciate our time together, it proved to me you cared.
Our life is like seasons and God created them all.
Winter, Summer, Spring and Fall, a place to hear your call.
Sometimes we don't want to listen, because of foolish pride,
But your feelings God does see, this you cannot hide.
In the quiet moments of the day, be silent and know,
This is the time our personality will begin to grow.
I pray you receive this truth I speak to you today,
For what would I gain, if I tell a lie, it only brings delay.
The consequence of life all comes together now,
So keep giving your heart till you can humbly bow.
You are a child of the King, Jesus is His name.
You see His love never changes, it always stays the same.

Trusts in the Lord

Faith
Hope
Lita
Paula
Pauline
Rachael
Rachel
Rae
Rochelle
Sabrina
Shella
Shellia
Thelma
Wendy
Wendi

Trustful Walks With God

You have a great big heart and little self esteem,
Put them both together, it makes a tremendous team.
Your tender heart reaches out wherever it can,
And your little self esteem keeps you humble as a lamb.
It's satisfaction for you depending on God for your source,
In all things be content, you will feel no remorse.
He sees you as a little child, looking to Him what is due,
Because you rely on Him and not what you can do.
God is big in your life and calls you His little lamb,
You know of his wisdom, He has counted each grain of sand.
God is mindful of all He has created and He really cares,
No wonder you rely on Him and are not afraid of snares.
Perfect peace go to them who put their trust in Him,
Yes, blessings are included, but your weakness He will trim.
For He sees you as you are and is mindful of your needs,
He'll bring you to a place of growing, just like a little seed.
You'll grow and grow till your capacity is full grown,
All will know you are a child of God by your love shown.
So rest in Him, your treasures are in heaven above,
Learn all you can to be ready with a perfect love.

Truth

Alicia
Alice
Alisa
Alica
Allison
Alison
Angela
Fushia
Jack
Jake
James
Jamie
Jacob
Jacqueline
Jim
Jimmy
Lexie
Lexey

Truthful

You do thirst to read the righteous law,
And seek each drop that Jesus saw.
So you will feel the affliction told,
Trials will come, bringing you forth as gold.
Don't be in despair, you are in tune,
Your praise is coming now to full bloom.
You will be calm no more to toss,
All because God's Son hung on the cross.
Just remember, we were all to blame,
But now you can call on Jesus' name.
Yes, He arose and life became anew,
Each victory you can claim and freedom, too.
You do thirst to read the righteous law,
And seek each drop that Jesus saw.
So get ready, the years ahead are much,
And you have a job of human love, to touch.
You shall peek through the darkest cloud,
And shall see the bright light in the crowd.
The light is the truth you look for,
Jesus will help you, you can be sure.
You will share each chance you meet,
To tell a soul their need to life complete.
Then no more a covenant you shall break,
For now you do live for Jesus' sake.

Victorious Life

Larry
Laura
Lora
Laurel
Laurie
Lori
Lavonne
Loraine
Loren
Laurette
Lorenza
Loretta
Luann
Luanne
Nicole
Vickie
Victoria

Victorious Life

Victorious spirit is what your name means,
That's why you find yourself dreaming new dreams.
God sees you as a queen and one to lead the way,
Remember to stay humble, its most important for you to stay
There is only one king, Jesus our Lord,
He spoke the Father's words, as His fighting sword.
Jesus is your Army to conquer each little war,
You will see results leading to a new open door.
A door to peace and contentment without bitterness and strife.
And seeing those around you happy in their life.
For He has put His mark on you, to show forth His seal,
This even gives you greater reason to have a burning zeal.
Yes, little daughter, you will be queen for the king of kings,
And one day He will call you, then you shall wear his ring.
Time is short prepare yourself, there is not time to waste.
Feast upon his word, which brings a heavenly taste.
Use your Bible as your sword and do as it is told;
Victory comes from fighting wars, using Jesus as your mold.
You will be a queen, keep fighting till you have won.
Thy Kingdom come in heaven and earth, thy will be done.

Victorious Spirit

Brandon
Burney
Clifford
Donald
Don
Larry
Lawen
Lawrence
Leourita
Lewis-Louis
Lorenzo
Luther
Nicholas
Ryan
Vance
Victor
Wade

Victorious Spirit

Victorious spirit is what your name means,
That's why you you find yourself dreaming new dreams.
You see yourself as king and one to lead the way,
Remember to be humble, it's most important for you to stay.
There is only one real king, He's Jesus our Lord,
He always used His Father's words, as His fighting sword,
Use Jesus as your army, to conquer each little war,
And you will see results, leading to a new open door.
A door to peace and contentment without bitterness and strife,
And seeing those around you happy in their life.
For he has put His mark on you to show forth His seal.
This even gives you greater reason to have a burning zeal.
Yes, my Son, you are a warrior for the greatest king,
And one day He'll call you, then you shall wear His ring.
Time is short prepare yourself. There is no time to waste.
You will feast upon His word, which brings a heavenly taste.
Use the Bible as your sword, and do as it is told.
Victory comes from fighting wars, using Jesus as your mold.
You are a warrior, keep fighting till you have won,
Thy kingdom come, in heaven and earth, Thy will be done.

Warrior

Cornelius
Garret
Ged
Gerald
Gideon
Gunda
Gunner
Lance
Marcus
Marcos
Perry
Peter
Philip
Reginald
Rodger
Roger
Ross
Skip

God's Warrior

A warrior for the King of Kings
Is your destiny for all things.
Jesus is His name, your Lord;
He and you with one accord.
There is a mighty battle against evil ways
Above the world, in prayer, you seem to always stay.
Giving all you have to fight the enemy,
God's grace to you He will abound to win the victory.
Face to face with Jesus is a perfect scene to see,
For he gives you paths to follow,
To stand against the enemy.
Principalities that we cannot see,
Who can win against this sin.
Jesus has won the battle, so keep in one accord,
It's only a matter of time for Jesus your Lord.
Sometimes lonely and worn out, too,
Just keep praying, He will see you through.
So be a warrior strong and true
That you might see His plan for you.
Your gift of songs to tell the story
Face to face, His steps of Glory.

Wisdom

Aldrich
Clark
Conrad
Con
Floyd
Harriet
Janice
Jean
Jeanette
Monica
Monique
Phoebe
Priscilla
Silas
Sonia
Sonya
Sophia

Full of Wisdom

Wisdom is a precious gift you own,
Many study to learn the unknown,
But you possess the secrect thought;
It's all inside just waiting to be sought.
Wisdom is far greater than all wealth
Use in matters for concern to health.
You found wisdom is the most important thing,
Wisdom the proven truth you cling.
A friend to treasure, you are one of a kind;
You brought me peace when I could not find.
Words are meaningful to you.
Why sometimes you feel blue;
Sensitive, while looking strong,
Others seem to take you wrong.
They don't know you need a friend,
And their time you need, if they could lend.
Generous with a giving heart,
You always exceed beyond your part.
All the giving is just a start
To all the wisdom within your heart.
The natural answers are yours inside,
The path of life, for you a guide.
So search inside the thoughts unknown,
Your gift from God, to show, you are his own.

Longsuffering

Luke 22:42-44

Jesus saying, Father if it be thy will, remove this cup from me: nevertheless not my will but thine be done, and being in agony he prayed and there appeared an angel unto him from heaven, strengthened him, and he prayed more earnestly: and his sweat was as it was great drops of blood falling down to the ground.

Forgiveness

Mark 11:25-26

And when ye stand praying, forgive if ye have sought against your brother or anyone: that your Father also which is in heaven may forgive you your trespasses.

But if you do not forgive, neither will your Father which is in heaven forgive your trespasses.

Worship

Matthew 4:10

Then said Jesus unto him, "Get thee behind me, Satan: for it is written, thou shall worship the Lord thy God, and Him only will thou serve."

John 4:23,24

But the hour cometh, and now is, when the true worshippers shall worship the Father in spirit and in truth; for the Father seeketh such to worship Him.

God is spirit, and they that worship Him must worship Him in spirit and in truth.

CONCLUSION

Christ has risen and He could not be kept in the grave. He has been resurrected in the hearts of lives today, of those that believe.

It is not by our success that we are measured or how intelligent we are. Christians are measured by who we are, the children of God.

Victories will be done in our life. Within our desires, to do the will of God. For its by his spirit and our awareness, that he leads His children to what He has created us to be.

If we keep our eyes on the creator instead of on what He created, we will not stray far from Him. We will be able to see Him as He is, Holy and the owner of everything here in this world. He will give wisdom to those who ask!

Jesus is the Son of God and He reigns. It was His prayer that we all become one, as He and the Father are one. Let us join Him in the prayer today.

JESUS CHRIST DIED FOR US.
JESUS CHRIST AROSE FROM THE GRAVE.
JESUS CHRIST WILL COME AGAIN.

About the Author

I was born September 15, 1938, Providence, Rhode Island. When I was nine years old, we left the east coast and moved to the west coast. We lived in California in the East Bay area. I finished my High School years in Richmond, California.

I married when I was twenty one years old to Robert Glemaker, and in the eighteen years we were married had four beautiful children, Deborah, Susan, Daniel, and David.

Jesus is my first love. And my children are the love of my life, who give me the reason to live. We lived the military life as my husband was in the Army. It was a good life but I was not living for the Lord at the time. I committed my life to serving the Lord Jesus Christ on November 7, 1974, at Ft. Benning, Georgia at a Kay Arthur Ladies Seminar. My friend Marsha Yearout led me to the Lord by bringing me to this particular Seminar.

We moved back to Fayetteville, North Carolina the summer of 1975, where we once lived while serving in the Army. After going through a trauma of divorce after eighteen years of marriage, I reached out to my Lord Jesus and His wisdom to raise my children. I served in the church as a teacher and sang in the choir and also served as Youth Director. I attended Stoney Point Baptist Church and Pastor Leon Humphrey was Senior Pastor. I am now attending Faith Temple, Ann and Richard Pia are Pastors. God has allowed me to change churches often due to moving around a lot. I find this good for me as I get to meet more of the Body of Christ.

The Holy Spirit has given me the strength to live each day for Jesus. My joy is in the Lord and His righteousness. I am not perfect only growing as a Christian daily.

The Lord inspired me to write this book December 16, 1985, which took me about a year to write. His love reaching out to any that will hear or draw near him.

About the Artist

Carletta (Letty Vaughn) Keith was born at Dale, South Carolina. She grew up on Cheeha Cambahee Plantation, near Waterloo, South Carolina. She is a self taught Artist and has won numerous awards since 1969, her work can be found in both public and private collections.

Carletta is not only a painter, she is also a silhouette Artist. She attributes her inspiration to try this Art to an old friend, Carew Rice. He lived at adjoining Brickhouse Plantation, she grew up admiring this man and his work. Mr. Rice passed away in May 1971 and Carletta did not forget her old friend or his Art.

One day Carletta, in March 1984, "inked" a piece of paper and cut her first silhouette. By the end of the day, she was hooked on her new-found Art, and felt strongly that she had found her "niche" in the Art field. Painting has since taken a back seat to her silhouettes and she feels that her old friend Carew is smiling and approving of her work as she cuts and snips pictures for all to enjoy.

Carletta and I have been friends for over twenty-four years and when I asked her to do the silhouettes for my book, she said these would be the first Biblical silhouettes she had done. After completing the work, she said she had enjoyed doing this work with me.

Carletta is talented in many areas in her life and has various hobbies. I like all of her work, but her silhouettes have a special place in my heart today.

Currently, Carletta resides in Cedar Creek, North Carolina with her husband Tommy and their daughter Jo.